Mystical
Courage

Mystical Courage

Commentaries on Selected Contemplative Exercises
by G.I. Gurdjieff, as Compiled by Joseph Azize

CYNTHIA BOURGEAULT

Red Elixir
Rhinebeck, New York

Paperback ISBN 978-1-954744-05-9
eBook ISBN 978-1-954744-06-6

Library of Congress Control Number 2021933766

Sections of *Gurdjieff: Mysticism, Contemplation, and Exercises* by Joseph Azize have been reprinted here by permission of Oxford University Press

Cover concept and photography by Andrew Breitenberg
Book layout by Colin Rolfe

Red Elixir is an imprint of Monkfish Book Publishing Company

Red Elixir
22 East Market Street, Suite 304
Rhinebeck, NY 12572
(845) 876-4861
monkfishpublishing.com

Contents

Introduction

In the Gurdjieff Work there is something called a "stop exercise." In the midst of a busy round of practical work, when people are fully engaged with whatever tasks they are doing, suddenly the team leader calls out, "STOP!" Everyone instantly freezes in place, caught midstream in whatever posture or gesture they happen to have assumed at that moment. It's an artfully diabolical learning tool, geared toward exposing the habitual repertory of unconscious mannerisms that keep us chained to our usual modes of self-presentation.

The pandemic that befell our planet late-winter 2020 looks to me in many ways like a gigantic, global *stop exercise*. By mid-March the whole world had essentially frozen in place. At brutal cost to human life, the complete severing of our usual rounds of unconscious frenetic activity was decisively accomplished. We stopped, cut off at the knees. But at least in my immediate, relatively privileged, circle of colleagues and Wisdom students, I was not seeing much movement toward part two of the exercise: the leaning into the awkwardness of that "caught-in-the-act" exposure to explore one's own repertory of habitual postures and attitudes that are somehow complicit in this mess. Instead,

I saw folks transitioning effortlessly—a little *too* effortlessly, it struck me—to online formats: Zoom lectures, Zoom conferences, even Zoom church services, in order to keep up the veneer of business as usual. The opportunity for a deeper kind of self-reckoning that might bear within it the seeds of genuine remorse and new beginning was being a bit sidestepped.

It was against that backdrop that I invited some of my experienced Wisdom students to work with six of the Gurdjieff Contemplative Exercises, now publicly available for the first time thanks to Joseph Azize's recently published book, *Gurdjieff: Mysticism, Contemplation, and Exercises*. Azize is an Australian student of the Work who first learned these exercises at the hands of his teachers George and Helen Adie, first-generation students of Gurdjieff himself.

I had had an earlier glance at the manuscript in late-fall 2019 during a small Work gathering in Dorset, and I was fortunate enough to be among the first to receive a published copy when the book became available in the United States in early January. I carried my copy along with me when I returned to London for an extended stay in February. My hosts were well-seasoned in the Work, with several decades of active duty in the School for Experimental Studies under their belts, and during our time together we worked our way through several of the exercises in the new Gurdjieff/Azize collection. It was an ideal first road test. We were all blown away, not only by the power of the exercises themselves but by a palpable sense of Gurdjieff's presence with us in the room, clearly willing to take the helm and directly guide our progress through the exercises.

When I got home in early March, just on the leading edge of all hell breaking loose, I wondered whether that same clear voice and steady presence at the helm might be willing to take on the navigation of a somewhat larger vessel—such as my worldwide network of Wisdom students, some of whom were similarly beginning to intuit a missing link, not only in the endless cultural chatter but even in the conventional resources of the Christian contemplative tradition.

That missing link is *embodied, three-centered awareness.* Embodied awareness not simply for the sake of personal wellness or mindfulness, *but as a direct link to higher faculties of perception embedded but not yet activated within us*—and through these "higher faculties"—to assistance coming toward us from worlds beyond our own. Among the many spiritual systems I have studied, Gurdjieff alone makes this assertion so categorically and teaches the foundational practices with such a comprehensive and clear trajectory.

The bottom line is simple: in the absence of a full, three-centered (thinking, feeling, moving) presence grounded in sensation and directed by conscious attention, we will inevitably default to thinking. And thinking is simply too low an energetic state to sustain the vision and connection we humans so desperately yearn for. We can talk, strategize, think, pray—even meditate—till the cows come home, but it is all on autopilot. The blind leading the blind. Gurdjieff is still, to my mind, the only one who is unequivocally stating this, and then showing us how to do the work.

And the tools are even more accessible now that that the exercises, the hidden "third pillar" of the Gurdjieff Work, are finally publicly available.

It will probably be obvious to sensitive readers that, in publishing his book, Jospeh Azize has carried out a fairly audacious raid on the temple, exposing to public scrutiny a significant collection of Gurdjieffian material that had formerly been transmitted only under close supervision within the inner sanctum of the Work. Its publication has caused justifiable distress to many faithful stewards of the Work across its various lineages, including people whom I cherish deeply as personal friends and mentors. And the risks of such broad exposure are indeed real: at the very least, vulgarization; more seriously, significant distortion and harm to a spiritual lineage which, despite its perhaps fatal siren call toward oversubtilization, has at least managed to cultivate an impressive level of Being among its maturing practitioners.

But with the cat now out of the bag anyway, it seemed like a missed opportunity not to call attention to this remarkable new resource, almost perfectly positioned to speak to the needs of our times if the proper introductions could be made. My Wisdom students were not exactly Gurdjieff neophytes; our on-the-ground Wisdom schools had already introduced them to those foundational Gurdjieffian concepts of three-centered awareness and conscious attention as well as to some of the basic protocols of inner work. Our Wisdom School Facebook community (where these commentaries first posted) was a closed group, offering some protection against uncontrolled access. Joseph Azize graciously agreed to make the exercises themselves available within the confines of the group, and thanks to a special licensing agreement with Oxford University Press, I am grateful to be able to extend that privilege still further. Each of the six exercises will appear at the beginning of the pertinent section of commentaries, allowing readers to follow the discussion more effectively—and more important, to actually try out the exercise for themselves. Please note, however, that only the "barebones" exercises are reproduced here, not Joseph Azize's exceedingly helpful notes and background material. To make maximum use of these commentaries, you will still need to acquire the Azize text itself—admittedly pricey, but in the long run well worth the investment. Along with the exercise itself, reproduced exactly from the Azize version, I have also included a reference to the pages in his text where the exercise is discussed.

I deliberately chose a conservative format for this exploration: written commentaries rather than an online study group. Not only does that better genre suit my own teaching style but it also continues a precedent already well established in the Work. The marvelous commentaries by Maurice Nicoll and J. G. Bennett are themselves works of deep reflection that extend both the scope and the subtlety of the original teaching. They have been a sturdy vehicle for both the wider transmission and deeper articulation of the Fourth Way tradition, and it is in their spirit that I offer my modest contribution here.

You will see immediately, however, that I am addressing a substantially different audience from those classic Work commentaries. The reflections gathered here are intended not so much for Gurdjieffian adepts (among whom I would hardly count myself) as for a broader spiritual audience starting primarily from Christian theological reference points. My intention here—as always—is to build a bridge connecting the dots between the familiar world of Christian contemplation and the brave new world of Gurdjieffian metaphysics and nomenclature, which I am nonetheless convinced is a wineskin entirely capable of bearing the good wine of their mystical Christian faith. Joseph Azize feels much the same way (he is, by the way, a Maronite priest). And his conviction that much of Gurdjieffian teaching is not only intrinsically mystical but also actively rooted in the Athonite tradition of Orthodox Christianity already establishes a compatible ground between his approach to these exercises and my own proclivities.

In their original iteration, these exercises were not a curriculum, let alone a standardized one. They were altogether "custom fitted," given to specific individuals or small groups in order to address specific developmental issues. They often arose impromptu, called forth by the situation itself. Once given, they became familiar traveling companions. Students would work on a single exercise for weeks or even months until what it had to offer had been fully assimilated. That is how Azize himself first learned them under the tutelage of George and Helen Adie. There was no established order or pedagogical trajectory. Certainly, no checklist.

I say this to acknowledge fully the inevitable misimpression that the present format creates. In collecting the exercises in the first place, rounding them up from the various lines of the Work and arranging them in chronological order, Azize may have already created this initial misimpression. But I have further compounded it, at least partially by intention. As I intuitively culled from among his basically three-dozen exercises a set of six that I thought would serve as a representative sampling, I began to realize that some deeper intelligence working inside me was already trained on the Four Ideals, one of Gurdjieff's final exercises and one which I intuited (rightly, I think) has deep healing potential for our planet exactly where it is pinned right now. While I hadn't started out with this objective in mind, it slowly revealed itself in the course of working with the material, and I watched as the other exercises arranged themselves like stepping stones, each one successively introducing essential skills while incrementally deepening the spiritual coherence of the whole. While I know full well that the exercises were not originally intended to form such a pattern, it was quite remarkable to discover that they would accommodate to such a pattern, allowing themselves to be shaped—as in their original iteration— to the direct need calling them forth.

In fact, as the impromptu "course" unfolded over about the six weeks bracketing either side of the Easter triduum, the perception began to grow that this whole wild experiment was somehow being guided from an intelligence beyond just our own. One participant specifically commented:

> I'm just amazed how such fine-tuned technology can be transferable and up and running in such a short space of time, across a Facebook page to, I am sure, a number of people like me who just a few weeks ago didn't have a clue. Step by step with each release of [new posts on] exercises gently bringing together mosaics of understanding and practicability that would normally take years to establish. Clearly there is power-assisted steering to all of this, something very high wants it to happen.

I suspect it was something on the order of "power-assisted steering" that my friends and I experienced so impressively as we gave these exercises (in their new format) that first London road test. The sense of Gurdjieff was still vibrantly present; still deeply attuned to the needs of our forlorn, lopsided planet; and still fully able to move in and shake up the playing field to connect with the needs of the times. This sense of his continuing presence is what ultimately gives me the confidence to say that this continuing experiment with the exercises, both Azize's and now my own, has been unconventional but perhaps not unwanted.

At any rate, the fruits of this experiment are now before you. I hope you find them good. Feel free to rearrange the pieces as you choose, allowing yourself to be drawn to the exercises that most deeply speak to you. Linger with them for as long as you want, and when and if you have given a good run to all of these initial six, remember that there are still nearly three dozen more awaiting you in Azize's book. With my blessing, and with his as well, have at it!

Approaching the Exercises:
The Foundational Pieces

Gurdjieff's forty or so "contemplation-like" exercises, developed gradually over three decades of teaching, are powerful tools of healing, cleansing, and clarity—and even when practiced individually or in small groups, they have a power to significantly shift our present planetary atmosphere. They are something you can actually *do* to steady yourself and ready yourself for the deeper energetic work that actually connects us and empowers us as a human species to accomplish the alchemical work we were placed on this planet to do.

The six exercises reproduced here are all examples of what Gurdjieff calls "transformed contemplation." For now—and in direct cognizance of the needs of our present global crisis—let me offer the following definition: Transformed contemplation is *contemplation that actually transforms something,* both in ourselves and in the world. It is a kind of sacred alchemy that is to be understood within the context of Gurdjieff's great vision of "reciprocal feeding," the exchange of physical/energetic substances between the realms that maintains the whole cosmic ecosystem in a state of dynamic equilibrium. We receive something for ourselves, we offer something back. Each of these exercises highlights a slightly different aspect of this and works on a slightly different skill set.

Before you dive in, you will need two foundational pieces:

1. A basic familiarity with the notion of three-centered awareness. This is part of the standard curriculum in my Introductory Wisdom Schools, but if you haven't been to Wisdom School—or simply want to refresh yourself—the gist of the teaching is also there in Chapter 3 of my *The Wisdom Way of Knowing.*

2. A familiarity with the basic body-rotation sensing exercise, which is foundational in the Gurdjieff Work and figures prominently in four of these five exercises. We have worked on this exercise a bit in the Introductory Wisdom School and extensively in the intermediate school (The Divine Exchange), but those of you who know me only as a teacher of Centering Prayer may not yet have been exposed to this particular practice. So here's the quick and dirty version:

> Further to SENSING; for the sake of this exercise, it means using your directed attention to awaken a sense of aliveness (often experienced as an actual subtle tingling) in a specific body part while at the same time allowing that part to be the full container for your attention.
>
> As a pilot run, bring your attention to your right hand. Try not to beam your attention down from outside, like a searchlight; rather, invite it gently to fill in from within. It will.
>
> Notice how, under the beckoning power of your attention, your arm suddenly seems to "come

online." You are directly connected to it; you feel its vibrancy as a vitalization of your own being. (Isn't it amazing how you can use this mysterious power always at your disposal, your attention, to fill up your hand with sensation; to increase the direct experience of your own aliveness?)

The rotation, then, typically goes: right arm, right leg; left leg, left arm. As your attention moves sequentially to each part, it also stays put there. If you see yourself wandering, daydreaming, judging—return to the direct sensation of the body part you are attending to.

For more on attention, have a look at "The Force of Attention" the marvelous excerpt by William Segal from his book *The Structure of Man.* You'll find bibliographical details at the back of this book.

With those two background pieces in place, you're good to go. Over the next few posts, I'll try to add a few further clarifying details and reflections about the specific exercises themselves.

The Clear Impressions Exercise

—Azize, pages 261–69

THE CLEAR IMPRESSIONS EXERCISE

1. The exercise is for a period of fifteen minutes. As you already know, the best time is the first thing in the morning .... This fifteen minutes is divided into three parts, and it makes very definite use of a clock. I want everybody to have a clock or a watch at hand. Not right in front of them, but at hand. And it's divided into three parts, that's five minutes each part.

2. And the first part is concerned with the outer impressions. And so, the first part, the eyes are open. In the second part it's concerned with the inner impressions, and the eyes are closed. And the third part, again, I am concerned with going back to the outer with as much realization as I can of myself, and also taking note of the outer, my obligations and plans for the day. And that's the third five minutes.

3. And the crux, the key difficulty, and also the maximum experience, the maximum new realization, comes exactly in the experience of taking in the visual surroundings. As I regard outside, I don't look in one spot. I take in everything that is in front of me, all my

surroundings, and everything in the surroundings, I take in.

4. But at the same time, I work on my sensation in rotation. A very extraordinary experience is possible there. I look, I take in the visual impressions. Of course, I also take in any sounds. But I take in the visual impression, but I do not stop this sensing in rotation.

5. The rotation order is one we're very familiar with: it's the right arm, the right leg, the left leg, the left arm, the area of the sex organs and spine, the solar plexus, and finally, the head. I sense in that order, one after another.

6. And I verify I have that sensation before I pass onto the next, *which is added*, so that I finally finish up with a *total* sensation.

7. In the meantime, I have an unbroken regard for the externals. And I look. Now what is going to take place there? I am not going to try and describe it now, but this is a very critical thing. You will be related to the outside world through your eyes. And yet, what will it mean?

8. I cannot lose any element of it. I am aware, I am working with my attention, and I am relaxing, and I am keeping my posture. Of course, I have to prepare before the fifteen minutes. I have to free myself, raise my arms, drop the belly, have a good posture. And then start. I maintain that posture, and I look around.

9. You will be in your own room. Your own room is full of objects: desirable, undesirable, tidy, untidy. And there you are. And your eye is going to see all of them, but you don't cease this effort. Now there is a very definite kind of effort, which you never ordinarily make. And somewhere between that are you.

10. And for the second five minutes, you close your eyes, and you relate to the inner scene. But you continue the sensing, you keep that. And you will see how the thoughts and associations of the inner country cannot proceed as usual. You have to judge that for five minutes. You can become quite accurate about it, without having to look up every half a minute.

11. And then the third five minutes: again, there's this outer contact, with visual impressions coming in. Once more, I keep sensing myself, coming to the sensation of myself as a whole. Then I get up and go to the day. It is finished.

12. What we need more than anything is to understand what we are about, so that all the moments of waking which we do have are not wasted. Many people have said that they have a moment of remembering, but they are in the void. And this is what I want you to experience: to be in the void.

13. See, when you are here with your sensation, and you have an impression, there's a confrontation. If you are present at the moment of confrontation, to that extent you are conscious.

14. The wrong kind of effort appears in the observations and reports ... Forcing is quite wrong; and yet we have to make effort. But what kind of effort? This exercise is to help us learn this effort.

15. Here's a note: "The essence of the exercise is to divide one's attention, to balance it, and to avoid tension and effort. This subtle effort is totally different from an ordinary idea of effort. The exercise is a very advanced and a very difficult one."

16. It is very simple, it's too simple for us. "If we try our best, we are certain this effort will not be wasted. Just

as all reality is one, so our subjective outer and inner
fantastic worlds are one, and it is between the reality
and the fantasy of both our inner and outer worlds
that our possibility of conscious development lies,
and where also lies the field of our work of becoming.
Actually in that between-situation."

17. That's where we want to come, and with the exercise, if
you fulfil it properly, you get the chance to experience
that between-situation."

18. Now in the experience of the exercise, in the first five
minutes, our eyes continually move and receive impressions of things external to us. As this continues, we
maintain our body sensing in rotation [Adie sets the
order out again], but we do not cease from regarding
our surroundings and all objects around us. However
we do not think about what we see, but try and keep
our recognition of what we see, in a way, in the background, very different from normal. Perhaps there will
seem to be *no* thoughts. The things we see seem to have
no significance. We do not possess them. We do not
understand them.

19. . . . and from this we could understand that always we
are caught and held, identified with what we see, and
that we project what we see. We *project* what we see,
creating for ourselves an unreal, fantastic world of pos-
sessions, demands, hates, lusts, irritability, and endless
appraisal and criticism.

20. And now, looking at these surroundings, they seem
to be different from usual, separated from us, we do
not understand them, and only with a special kind
of felt effort can we continue to sense ourselves and
at the same time receive these impressions external to us; receive them without identification. This

is a confrontation, leading perhaps to a moment of self-awareness, a moment of consciousness ... not *seeing*, but of consciousness.

21. And don't forget that in the last five minutes, we try and sense ourselves, inner and outer, simultaneously. And we continue to sense ourselves. So let us try now . . .

22. . . . The movement of sensing can be regular. The taking in of impressions can be irregular. Perhaps you find a cessation of words . . . and yet I couldn't say that I am less aware of where I am.

23. Some people tend to have a fixed stare. Don't do that. Move your eyes. More difficult, but it will stop you getting tense. Don't fear to take in everything.

24. Now the second five minutes . . . . I am present to my body and my sensation. Comments are very faint, they're in the background. This guarding, and the sensing of the limbs in this order, this isn't thought, this isn't like any other thoughts. I am able to do that without thinking. See, there's some element in me, my higher mind—it can function without all those words. I can know if I slow down.

25. I am also aware of feeling, my feeling. I also maintain my posture . . . .

26. Before I open my eyes, I listen to the reverberation. "I" . . . "Am." [Those present repeat "I" . . . "Am."]

27. The third period starts. I retain this rotation of sensation. I retain the feeling.

28. . . . I am in this position, being present to the visual and audible impressions: what are my plans for the day? I haven't lost my sensation. I know I am here. What is left for me but some flashing idea of the kind of day,

the kind of trap; what I may need; that to which I have
to return, but not as I was, not a slave.

29. I can have inner presence and speak and look. Why
should I not? This is to experience that.

30. Again, with the eyes open, I experience that vibration:
"I" . . . "Am." [They respond again.] It is freer, the "I"
. . . "Am" is freer.

On October 29 or 30, 1980, Adie gave the exercise
again, but this time he reversed the order of the first two
parts, commencing with the eyes closed. I shall set out only
those parts of the instructions that complement what was
said previously. I shall continue the numbering, although
these comments are from a different meeting.

31. Of course the eyes are relaxed. They are not strained
at all. The face is relaxed in all parts. I visit everything.
I am busy. I begin to get a sense of another point from
which I am working. Something central.

32. As I pass from point to point, I begin to establish
awareness of the relativity within me, which leads to a
beginning of the sense of wholeness, the oneness.

33. This is a very relaxed position. For me, perhaps, I had
the idea that with my eyes open it would be tense. Not
at all. It's just a window open, nothing more. I work
here, and I am open to *that* level.

34. Because if I experience or relate to that level at all, I
realize that that level must be in me. I can only recognize it, respond to it from an equal level. Not to think
too much about that . . .

35. When the visual impressions, the forces enter, I receive
these without words. I freely turn my head from one
side to the other, up and down . . . I may receive

impressions which I haven't had since I was a young child. But I don't think about anything. I am free from thought, and to ensure this, as I turn my head with the windows of my eyes open, receiving impressions without words or explanations . . . I maintain a series of sensations of my limbs . . .

Afterwards, he added this note:

36. Like this, one may experience real struggle to retain an inner balance. It is like being in a whirling machine. They have such machines in the training of pilots and astronauts, simulators, going into a vehicle free of gravity. In this situation, one tries to establish an inner center of gravity, which effects the blood flow, and it directs the consciousness away from the head towards the compelling reactions and even the visceral sensations of the bowels.

37. This is such a definite, and at the same such a demanding exercise, like creating your own center of gravity, the sense of level and direction, while all these coordinates are moving, in this one may have a very brief moment of effort with actually no attention left for normal thought. From such an experience, a self-awareness is possible, and the cutting of the momentum of ordinary dreams and associations.

38. From this one can face a clean, new, strange unknown day, of more conscious life, from which the possibility of some kind of will-action involved in purpose, choice, will and fulfilment becomes possible; and the fulfilment is always more and different than one can imagine in the planning.

COMMENTARY

The Clear Impressions Exercise is perhaps the most accessible of these six exercises for those of you starting from known reference points in Centering Prayer. It's a quieter, more passive (if you want to call it that) kind of Gurdjieffian exercise in which you are not making a strenuous effort with either the imagination or the will but simply allowing yourself to take in what comes into sight (either outwardly or inwardly) without judgment or reactivity. The receptive attitude may feel vaguely familiar—and you even get to keep your eyes closed for five minutes!

But the exercise also catapults you straight to the core of what Gurdjieff means by "transformed contemplation": the full, vibrant, sensation-based participation of the body in the exercise. Unlike Centering Prayer (and most entry-level meditation practices on all paths, whether they be "concentrative methods," "awareness methods," or "receptive methods" according to Thomas Keating's popular schematic), *you are not trying to make the body neutral here*; rather, you intentionally engage its full, vibrant, sensation-based participation, both as a way of energizing your own presence and as a way of balancing and grounding your attention so that it is less likely to veer off into mental channels.

In Gurdjieffian teaching, the three "being foods" required for our participation in life are food, air, and impressions. To the extent that we ingest these in a state of conscious presence (i.e., balanced in all three centers) they not only sustain our physical body but begin to crystallize more subtle bodies within us that allow us to participate in those more subtle realms (like the imaginal!) from which deeper wisdom and sustenance are always flowing.

The main roadblock here is our over-reliance on thinking, which usurps three-centered awareness and lowers the level of our being without our even noticing. This exercise, if you stick with it, will expose that roadblock and help you cut through it.

As you work your way around the body rotation, simultaneously taking in the impressions that present themselves to you, you'll notice how often your attention defaults to thinking and how the head takes over as the unconscious command center of your being. Try not to wince. For you'll also taste a whole different quality of vibrancy and awareness when you manage to stay balanced and grounded in sensation. You'll begin to taste how thinking—no matter how brilliant or inspired—is always one-dimensional, flat, stale. Presence is something of an entirely different order.

This exercise is based on the basic body rotation I introduced in my last post but adds a new triad: sexual organs and spine, solar plexus, head. It's quite a wake-up call (for me, anyway) to experience my head *through sensation*—its weight, balance, buzziness as thoughts fly by—and not get lured back into thinking.

The "eyes closed" part of this exercise is bookended by "eyes open" parts in which you keep your head moving slightly (not fixed on a point) and allow yourself simply to notice what comes into sight. There's an almost irresistible temptation to name or inventory. Try not to. You may also notice when something you see hits one of your inner nerve points and starts to throw you into action—like the mug left on the coffee table hissing at you, "*untidy,*" siren-calling you to get up at once and remove it to the sink. Try not to, but do notice the strength of the impulse.

The inner part is the same drill. Eyes closed, but now it is the thoughts that steal in on little cat's feet. Just let them be, like the mug on the coffee table.

For me, the great experiential learning in this exercise is exactly as Azize's teacher, George Adie, describes it in #19:

> And from this we could understand that always we are caught and held, identified with what we see, and we *project* what we see. We project what we see, creating for ourselves an unreal, fantastic world of possessions, demands, hates, lusts, irritability, and endless appraisal and criticism.

Not for the faint of heart. But in that seeing, a shackle snaps loose, and a different kind of energy rushes in. For a few minutes, the world is a distinctly different place.

The Lord Have Mercy Exercise

—Azize, pages 241–49

A "Lord Have Mercy" exercise was given by George Adie on February 20, 1980. The entire instruction took approximately twenty minutes, beginning with a prologue:

1. We have to move. It's like the practice of the presence of God.
2. We have to *move* to the *fact* of the awareness of higher forces, the awareness of what is going on outside without leaving the place.
3. I am here with you, you're with each other, everybody together. But there is something else.
4. I don't *think* about it, but still I am aware of it; it's a possibility. And as I move toward that possibility, that expansion of consciousness, of course I begin to get all that I need. Let us take the exercise.

Adie then spent some time speaking about the proper physical posture to be taken for the exercise.

5. That wants to be done very frequently, because all life is producing other tense postures.
6. Now the exercise, the sitting, the preparation. I need to

understand how essential preparation is. Preparation is the determiner of the moment that follows, which determines the future. If there is any possibility, it cannot take place without preparation. If I am not conscious now, then I have much less chance of receiving any impulses later, or of noticing them.

7. I wish to prepare.

8. One of the main interferences, in fact one of the key interferences: the words in the head. The head is not related to the body, the head is separate, turning in dreams and imagination . . . and identification. Quite unaware of the body, even though I was putting it in posture.

9. So now I try and have an all-over sense in myself, an all-over sense of myself without any words. I want to free my head. Free it from words. Connect it to my body.

10. And now I keep part of the attention, not all of it, on this awareness, my total awareness, and my total freedom from words. I remain, and I place the other half of my attention on my right arm. And I *sense* my right arm: I sense it. I have no words, and I sense the arm.

11. I start maybe at the top, and go down to the bottom, but . . . if I have done a lot of sensing and exercise in the past, I find that the arm is there rather readily. What I need is a finer sensation, not just peripheral, I need a total sensation of the arm, the fineness, the life flowing in that arm.

12. And as I sense the arm, I have the concept, as if I said to myself: "Lord have mercy."

13. Perhaps I must start innerly. It's as if I innerly said: "Lord have mercy." But you see, it's still there. I don't

have to repeat, I don't even have to repeat the *thought* of the words "Lord have mercy."

14. They echo in me without repeating them. I sense my arm. In me is the echo: "Lord have mercy."

15. Now with that sensation, which I don't leave, I then pass to the right leg, and again: "Lord have mercy." I experience, I sense the life force in that limb, and in the body . . . my central presence free from any words, and the right arm . . . and the right leg.

16. And now I sense the left leg. Again: "Lord have mercy." Again it echoes there.

17. When I have established a really fine sensation in that leg, I pass to the left arm. Again: "Lord have mercy." I. Central. Free from thought. All limbs with the force in them, sensed. And this wordless echo: "Lord have mercy." I experience the influence of the words.

18. Now, in my own time, I repeat that series of four movements again. And then a third time, each time getting finer.

19. When I have finished this series, I have a total experience of myself. Total. The whole. The presence of the whole, the reality of my conscious being, and in me: "Lord have mercy."

20. I remember that. I have no words, no thoughts.

After this, there followed about five minutes of silence. Adie then asked:

21. When I open my eyes, can I receive the impressions without words?

After another minute, he said:

22. Enough.

23. For this maximum withdrawal, for this maximum protection of this effort, one should close the eyes. Several people are inclined not to.

24. That preparation should rightfully take about fifteen minutes, about five or seven minutes to really have that experience, and then you remain quite free from words of any sort.

25. After that, you can't leap from your chair. You then have a moment or two, at least, to put your mind on your intention for the day. You may have thought about it previously and have it there. And then you go. You have to plunge into life after that.

26. There would be no virtue in this exercise, and you shouldn't receive very much from it, unless it's going to be aimed at a purpose. The whole is that I shall have the power to do, the power to discriminate, the power to *act* even, with intention. For this which we have been practicing is an act, an inner act. Now I wish to be able to have something related to that in my life.

27. And now, as we listen to the music, let us listen again, without words.

Helen Adie's Version

This transcript is taken directly from a handwritten draft of Helen Adie's. It is a not unimportant supplement to the above as it records what she evidently considered to be a reliable and full, if concise, text of the exercise. When such exercises are given extempore, there is both a risk of something being overlooked and the possibility that a fresh aspect will be discovered and brought.

After establishing sensation, concentrate on feeling (as in *I Am*). Then connect that feeling with feeling in the arms and especially with the words *Lord Have Mercy*. Order for limbs which are in canon—

1. right arm, right leg, left leg, left arm
2. right leg, left leg, left arm, right arm
3. left leg, left arm, right arm, right leg.

Then with the reverberation *I Am*.

Finally, remain within own atmosphere, keeping emanations within that limit—watching the breathing—taking in the higher hydrogens with the in-breath, and retaining them with the out-breath for at least <u>five minutes</u>.

The main difference between this and the exercise given by her husband is that in this exercise the entire round of the four limbs is gone through four times; in canon. Also of significance is the remaining for five minutes or more after the exercise, continuing the breathing exercise, because it shows that the exercise is valued partly because of the state it produces. Once more, it makes a connection between this prayer and Gurdjieff's own invocation: "I am."

COMMENTARY

1. The Importance of Embodiment

Let me begin today's commentary with a pithy reminder from my dear friend A. H. Almaas as to the fundamental importance of these sensory embodiment exercises:

The body is the doorway to the adventure of Being. So the inquiry has to begin by activating and enlivening the body. The more active and alive the whole body is, the more our inquiry is vital and our unfoldment is alive. Our experience is more robust, energetic, and dynamic. We need to remember that the activation of the *lataif* [the subtle senses of perception in Sufi tradition, allowing us to peer directly into the invisible realms] requires that the centers of physical location be energized (Almaas, 294).

In the absence of a vibrant, awakened presence in our physical body, we default to thinking without even knowing we are doing it. Then everything becomes a projection of the story inside our heads, including (tragically) our deepest sense of our own aliveness.

All meditation traditions recognize that nothing real can happen to us while we are still trapped in the mind. But most try to deal with this by simply "turning off the mind," or replacing thought with some idealized emotional state (such as peace, bliss, calm). What is distinctive about the Gurdjieffian system is that it goes in the opposite direction, engaging the full aliveness of the body to contain and counterbalance the mind while at the same time raising the frequency of our presence to a vibrational level where direct perception begins to become possible.

In his introductory remarks on the Lord Have Mercy Exercise, George Adie cuts straight to heart of the problem in his instructions #8 and #9: "The head is not related to the body, the head is separate, turning in dreams and imagination ... and identification .... I want to free my head. Free it from words. Connect it to my body" (Azize, 245).

Whether you work with the basic form of this exercise given by George Adie or the slightly more complex variation offered by his wife, Helen, (both included here), the exercise itself is fairly straightforward. It's the straight-up, four-point body rotation: right arm, right leg, left leg, left arm—executed either three times (George's version) or four (Helen's). The plot twist here is that simultaneously with the sensation itself, you *gently* add the words, "Lord Have Mercy."

"Gently" means that this is not a mechanical repetition of an external prayer—but rather, almost "an echo," as George Adie describes it. And "gently" also means that you are not imposing a liturgical formula from the outside, laying onto the exercise a devotional patina. Rather, you are *gently* opening a question (whose essence is in fact a petition): Is it possible to become directly aware of the subtle relational field that in fact surrounds us at all times and is the ground of our own aliveness—the Mercy of God?

The depth of feeling this simple exercise can evoke is stunning. Something can indeed be directly tasted here, a something which opens the heart while at the same time verging on breaking it. A sense of yourself as "the thou of an I" (in Ramon Panikkar's words), infinitely fragile and precious—while at the same time a poignant draught of "the sorrow of our common Father" (Gurdjieff's words).

2. Lord Have Mercy and the Jesus Prayer

Azize drives the point hard that Gurdjieff's Lord Have Mercy Exercise has its origin in the Jesus Prayer (or "Prayer of the Heart") of the Orthodox Church, particularly in the Athonite tradition (the monastic mystical traditions tended by the monks of Mount Athos). I must admit that I am not fully convinced by his arguments. It seems clear that the root of Gurdjieff's deep resonance with the phrase "Lord have mercy" (which shows up again and again in his work, not just in the exercises but also in the movements, in *Beelzebub's Tales to his Grandson*, and in his own more openly orthodox religiosity during the last years of his life) emanates not in the Jesus Prayer ("Lord Jesus Christ, only son of God, have mercy on me a sinner") but in the Trisagion—that triune invocation of the threefold name of God, which is a bedrock of Orthodox mysticism:

> *Holy God*
> *Holy and mighty*
> *Holy immortal one,*
> *Have mercy on us…*

Or in the Greek form, which he would have sung as a choir-boy during his years at the cathedral school in Kars:

> *Agios Ô theos*
> *Agios iskyros*
> *Agios athanotos*
> *Eleison imas …*

Gurdjieff refers to this prayer extensively in "The Holy Planet Purgatory," his sweeping cosmogonic exposition which ends the Second Book of *Beelzebub's Tales*. The triune God is at once the Trinity and the Law of Three, the two of them joined at the hip. For attuned readers, you'll see that he even alludes to the Greek version in his otherwise "nonsensical" nomenclature on page 687, describing these three forces as "surp-oth-eos" (Ô *Theos*), "surp-skiros" (*Iskyros*), and "surp-athanotos" (*Athanotos*). Gurdjieff's "Lord" is irreducibly a Trinitarian, cosmogonic, personal, law-of-three relational field in which all is held together, given life and breath in the fundamental exchange that is the source of the entire created order. The Mercy is its shape, its color, its substantiality, and it can be tasted directly *when perceived directly in the awakened heart, grounded in an enlivened bodily presence.* That is definitely the pot of gold awaiting at the end of this rainbow in this exercise.

To try to capture the spaciousness of this feeling within the classic Jesus Prayer, (whose take-off point is the invocation of a particular person within the Trinity) is, in my estimation, to hold it too tightly. Jesus does not figure prominently in Gurdjieff's own devotional mysticism (nor for that matter does the anatomical heart, around which the Athonite mysticism gravitates so powerfully). For Gurdjieff, Jesus is definitely one of the highest attained sacred individuals sent to offer aid, but he is on the order of other such cosmic helpers and messengers (like Buddha and Muhammed)—not an ontological singularity. Jesus is a finger pointing at the moon; rather than looking directly *at* Jesus, *Gurdjieff looks in the same direction as Jesus and sees what Jesus sees*: the broken heart and deep sorrow of "our common Father" as He continuously takes into His own heart the anguish and fracturedness which is the shadow side of all manifestation.

The real resonance in this exercise is not so much with the Jesus Prayer as with Gurdjieff's own Fourth Obligolnian striving (*Gurdjieff*, 352): "from the beginning of one's existence to pay as quickly as possible for one's arising and individuality in order afterward to be free to lighten as much as possible the sorrow of our Common Father."

And it is this same striving, which I believe offers the most spacious container for holding the otherwise almost unbearable tenderness that flows through this otherwise mysteriously simple exercise.

3. From the Jesus Prayer to the Prayer of the Heart

There is indeed a way to connect the dots between Gurdjieff's version of Lord Have Mercy and the Jesus Prayer of Orthodox Hesychasm. But the route doesn't lie through their formal or theological similarities. You have to dive down deeper, to their common ontological core.

Azize properly calls attention to a statement made in *The Reality of Being* by Jeanne de Salzmann (Gurdjieff's designated lineage bearer) that the phrase, "I AM"—surely one of the core mantras in the Gurdjieff teaching—can be replaced with the phrase "Lord have mercy." I would personally be far more cautious than Azize in reading implications into this statement. From *The Reality of Being* text itself (de Salzmann, 73) it is not clear whether this is general principle of equivalency sanctioned by Gurdjieff himself, or a situational dispensation granted by de Salzmann. But my gut feeling is that that the awareness of a deep reciprocity between these two statements does in fact originate with Gurdjieff himself. It is certainly not alien to his spirituality and may in fact be at the heart of it. And when you follow his lead here, it winds up revealing some surprising new depths in both the I Am and the Lord Have Mercy.

At these depths, by the way, it doesn't really matter whether you hear this phrase as emanating from the Trisagion or the Jesus Prayer. In the end, the two prayers are two streams of the same river.

CHRISTOPHANY...

To make this deeper inquiry into the meaning of the phrase Lord Have Mercy and why it might even remotely be considered an equivalent to the affirmation I AM, you will need two resources, which thankfully will already be familiar to many of you in the Wisdom Community. The first is Raimon Panikkar's *Christophany: The Fullness of Man*—specifically, section two, "The Mysticism of Jesus the Christ" (pp. 39–138).

The second is Olga Louchakova's extraordinary 2004 essay, "Essence of the Prayer of the Heart," which has circulated in Xerox copies for many years within our Wisdom community but is also easily available online. (My page numbering follows the original published version as a chapter in a collection of poetry by spiritual teacher Lee Lozowick, called *Gasping for Air in a Vacuum*.)

In his powerful reflection on Jesus's own deepest sense of selfhood, Panikkar is struck by two apparently contradictory aspects: first, Jesus's "intense sense of filiation," as Panikkar calls it, encapsulated in the phrase, "Abba, Father!"; second, his serene sense of connaturality with his divine source, exemplified in the phrase "I and my Father are one." Jesus experiences himself as both finite and infinite, temporal and timeless, dual and nondual. These two poles of his being are not static; rather, they become the driveshaft of a dynamic, relational ground held together by the continuous act of kenotic self-giving, summarized in Panikkar's memorable one-liner: "I am one with my source insofar as I, too, act as a source by making everything I have received flow again." This is the sphere of the Person, in which God becomes recognizable as love.

AND LOUCHAKOVA ...

Olga Louchakova's brilliant study of the Jesus Prayer brings together her extensive knowledge of the Vedanta and yogic traditions as well as her own initiation in a contemporary Russian school of Hesychasm. Her approach is comparative and phenomenological, taking Prayer of the Heart as a type of spiritual self-inquiry which boldly poises itself on the cusp between dual and non-dual experience, affirming the validity of both while linking them in precisely the same dynamic flow we have already observed in Panikkar's exegesis.

"Prayer of the Heart is implicitly a dialog," she writes, "it is relational, always I-thou" (Louchakova/Lozowick, 43). But the nature of that dialogue is not static, not simply the petition of a hapless mortal to a divine power-broker (as many still hear in the phrase, "Lord Jesus Christ, have mercy on me"). Rather, tenaciously anchored in the *embodied sense of self carried in the chest*—and she insists on this!—it morphs into a deepening self-inquiry and finally into a *"whole being engagement in the direct perception of identity"* (Ibid., 39). When followed all the way to its endpoint, Prayer of the Heart marks a journey that "collects the self, transcends the self, annihilates the self, then annihilates the annihilation."

In the end, one discovers it is not merely the individual identity that is being systematically onion-skinned; we find ourselves partaking in a parallel process within the layers of divine identity as well, until at last we find ourselves standing at the very precipice of that cosmic wormhole through which the divine Unmanifest is forever pouring itself into form. As Louchakova remarkably writes, "The practitioner becomes aware of the innermost mystery of the ontopoietic (self-manifesting) process" (Ibid., 47).

And one final gorgeous insight:

> This continuous [repetition of the name of the Divine Person], accompanied by the inward flow of worship in the direction of intimacy with the unknown other, opens the focus on the origins of Being .... This engagement with the unknown God-Other is the pivotal moment where the emotion of love loses its willed

direction and becomes a continuum, a field .... The individual self does not cease to exist; it is not voided, but becomes a locus of the manifestation of the larger life.

That field—that dynamic flowing continuum between finite and infinite—is what Panikkar senses as the essence of the mind of Christ. It is also a pretty good felt-sense approximation of what Gurdjieff means by "Lord have mercy." And remember, if you will, that venerable insight from Helen Luke's iconic book, *Old Age*, that the word "mercy" originates in an old Etruscan root whose meaning is "*exchange*." Just like in "commerce" and "mercantile."

CONNECTING THE DOTS

Once that continuous backdrop of exchange is recognized, it is not difficult to connect the dots between the Lord Have Mercy, the Jesus Prayer, and the I AM. They join precisely at that "innermost mystery of the ontopoietic process."

Gurdjieff, Panikkar, Jesus, and the Jesus Prayer all implicitly recognize that Being—by which I mean not just our individual being but divine Beingness itself—arises within a relational field. *It is nobody's ontological possession, not even God's.* "I AM" is not an *a priori* assertion, not a statement that can be made or even cognized apart from that field. The spiritual modality being shared here is not the "atman is Brahman" mode, not a non-dual realization that cancels all particularity. Rather it is a supremely Western acknowledgment of and self-entrustment to the coherence and dynamism of that relational field.

To the degree that Louchakova is correct in the assertion that the Orthodox Prayer of the Heart has at its epicenter the burning quest to discover and abide in that true I AM, then I think the affinity between this tradition and the mainspring of the Gurdjieffian teaching becomes evident.

But to say that the two terms "I AM" and "Lord Have Mercy" are equivalents, that they can be used interchangeably, is to say something still more: that they invoke each other, that they are each implicit in the other, "bidden or unbidden."

For me, this radically shifts the picture, makes me hear both phrases with new ears.

Whenever I say, "I Am"—as within Helen Adie's version of the Lord Have Mercy Exercise, at the sectional divisions in the Clear Impressions Exercise, or the Make Strong, it is with the implicit recognition that this is not about me finding *my* Real I, "my" realized being. It is all going on within the wondrously mysterious and irreducible sphere of the divine Mercy. One bows the knee of the heart.

When I say, "Lord have mercy," I am not making a pious devotional statement. It's not about worthy or unworthy, shame and guilt, blame and punishment. Rather, I am feeling to my very bones that yearning for being and sharing of being that permeates the entire created order. I am implicitly acknowledging that one cannot know without also *being known*. I am affirming my willingness to stay awake, to endure the vulnerability. I am actively engaging humility—not obsequiousness, but a recognition of the scale of things, the depth of the suffering and the yearning that binds the created order to the uncreated light.

Jesus is the tie-rod holding the I AM and the Lord Have Mercy together. That is Panikkar's point. And hence, whether there is or is not a *formal* connection between Gurdjieff's Lord Have Mercy Exercise and the Athonite traditions of Orthodox monasticism, there is definitely a heart resonance there, a path that will become increasingly clear as the exercises take root in your own heart.

"Make Strong! Not Easy Thing" Exercise

—Azize, pages 178–82

"MAKE STRONG! NOT EASY THING" EXERCISE

This exercise was found in Yale University's Beinecke Rare Manuscripts Library among the papers of Jean Toomer. Dated 1939, it has been accepted as authentic by many in the Gurdjieff groups, and it is entirely of a piece with Gurdjieff's exercise. The version published in 2014 includes a postscript in which the writer states that it was given to him or her from Gurdjieff (paragraph 11 below).

1. Fifteen minutes relax. Break tempo of ordinary life before doing exercise.
2. Breath in—"I." Breath out—"am." With all three parts do. Not just mind. Feeling and body also. Make strong! Not easy thing.
3. When breathe out, imagine part of air stays in and flows to corresponding place. Where flow, how flow, that is its business. Only feel that part remains.
4. Before beginning exercise say: "I wish to keep this substance for myself."

5. Without this conscious and voluntary labor on your part nothing at all will be coated. All will in time evaporate.

6. Just this small property in blood makes possible very big result if done with conscious labor. Without this, for one month you must work for such result.

7. When doing, must be very careful not to change exterior. It is inner thing. No one need know. Outside keep same exterior. Inside you do.

8. Not hold breath. Just breathe in and out. Of course, to change thinking will take time. Automatically breath will adjust.

9. To be able to do exercise not lopsidedly you must put whole attention on it. To arouse feeling, interest, and attention for cooperation you must think the following before beginning: "I am now about to begin this exercise. With full attention I will draw in my breath, saying 'I,' and sensing the whole of myself. I wish very much to do this in order that I may digest air."

10. To arouse body to cooperate, take corresponding posture. Inner tension of forces. Mobilize your centers for working together for this aim. In breathing [out] imagine something flows, like when inhaling cigarette.

11. I am now about to begin this exercise, which I have been fortunate enough to learn from Mr. Gurdjieff, and which will enable me with the aid of conscious labor, to coat higher bodies in myself from active elements in the air I breathe.

COMMENTARY

I was first introduced to this exercise by my dear colleagues Amy Silver and Deborah Rose Longo at Claymont. We worked with it during both sessions of our Gurdjieff /Teilhard seminar last fall, where it definitely raised the collective fineness of our group ("fineness" here being understood as sensitivity, vibrancy, and synergy).

This exercise is particularly beloved by many Work devotees because it speaks in Gurdjieff's own voice and thus bears his presence in a particularly personal and sacramental way. (It seems to have been copied down essentially verbatim by one of his students, preserving not only his instructions but also his broken English and his unique pacing and syntax.)

In this exercise we will be working primarily with the breath—though inseparable, of course, from its other two major components, the I AM carried on the breath and the three-centered awareness.

For Gurdjieff, breathing was the source of our second "being food," which not only sustains life in the planetary body, but also contains—if the breathing is conscious and fully embodied—elements needed for the building up of our subtle inner bodies, the bodies that allow us to begin *here and now* to perceive and navigate in the invisible higher realms. Without trying to hold the terms too tightly, the gist of the idea is laid out in a couple of key paragraphs in Gurdjieff's chapter called "Hypnotism" in *Beelzebub's Tales* (520–21):

> The substances of that part of the being-blood
> designed by Nature for serving the planetary body
> arise from the transformation of the substances of that
> planet on which the given being is formed and exists.

> But the substances designed for serving the *kesdjan*
> body of the being, which in their totality are called
> "*hanbledzoin*," are obtained from the transformation of

elements of other planets and of the sun itself of that system where this three-brained being has the place of his arising and existence.

Finally, that part of the being-blood which almost everywhere is called the sacred "*aiëssakhladonn*," and which serves the highest part of the being called the "soul," derives from the direct emanations of our Most Holy Sun Absolute [i.e., the Source of Everything existing, or God Himself].

After explaining that the substances required for the building up of our planetary body are ingested in the form of food, and for our first higher body (the kesdjan body) from breathing, he then adds the kicker:

As for the sacred cosmic substances required for the coating of the "highest being-body," which they call the "soul," these substances can be assimilated and correspondingly transformed and coated in them only through the process of what is called "aiësiritoorassian contemplation," actualized in their common presences with the conscious participation of their three independent spiritualized parts [i.e., their three centers].

Aiesiritoorassian Contemplation is the term that Azize translates throughout his study as "transformed contemplation." If you take the *"aiëss"* cognate seriously, it literally means "contemplation intended to nourish the sacred *aiëssakhladonn*, which emanates directly from God and builds up our highest being body, the soul. This is what these exercises *in toto* are all about. They contain the heart of Gurdjieff's vision of transformation and the essence of his method for how to get there.

As we work with this exercise it is important to bear in mind that we are actually taking in a substance gratuitously offered to us through the mercy of God for the building up within us of that "immortal diamond" which allows us to live here and now in those deeper waters that lie beyond death. We could all use a bit more of that substance on our planet just now!

"NOT EASY THING..."

The second component in this exercise is the I AM, which is placed on the breath: "I" on the in-breath, "am" on the out-breath.

We have already explored in my last commentary how I am and Lord Have Mercy are essentially functional equivalents for Gurdjieff; they invoke and complete one another. I AM is not an autonomous assertion of "my" individual being; it arises within a relational field as a gift mysteriously given in each moment. The name of this field is The Mercy, and as I have been pointing out for twenty years now (borrowing an insight from that venerable wisewoman Helen Luke), the root of the old Etruscan term mercy—*merc*—literally means "exchange." It has nothing to do with pity, let alone condescension. It speaks of flow.

"Every breath you take is the breath of God," the wise old monk Theophane of Snowmass was fond of saying. We sense this gift freely flowing toward us, and realize that we do not hold ourselves in life; it is renewed in us, breath by breath. Try to sense The Mercy as you say the I AM; let them dance in one another. And if you want, ponder this comment Gurdjieff made: "When I say *I*, something inside me stands up; when I say *AM*, something inside me sits down." If you recall Olga Louchalova's insight (in my last commentary) about standing on the threshold of "innermost mystery of the ontopoietic (self-manifesting) process"—well, there you are!

As your inner sensing gets more subtle, you may actually begin to be directly aware of these higher-being substances as they play in the air you take in. Just in the moment before the out-breath draws back into in-breath, you may sense them particularly pungently. But don't strain to catch it, and above all—*don't mess with your breathing!* Don't pause or add in any artificial hesitations. Gurdjieff was strictly adamant in breathing exercises that the natural flow of the breathing not be interfered with. It is a very good precaution, for both safety and humility.

MAKE STRONG!

"Make strong!" means to do this exercise in all three centers; if you float through it on autopilot, nothing will have been gained. While this exercise does not involve a body rotation., Gurdjieff does call for an initial "fifteen-minute relax"; during this time, it would not be time ill-spent to summon your bodily presence to full attention. Get yourself alert, collected, and filled with sensation. Then you'll be good to go.

The task of the intellectual center is to keep the mind from wandering; the emotional center becomes engaged as you realize the sacredness of the being-sustenance you are being offered and feel the Mercy of God as an intimate enfolding tenderness holding you and everything else together.

At this exact moment, as we enter the eye-of the needle of Holy Week surrounded by a global pandemic, I am excruciatingly aware of the corporate and collective dimension of this exercise. When the COVID-19 virus kills, it kills by taking away the capacity to draw nourishment from this second being-food, the air. I breathe in solidarity with all those struggling for breath; I feel that the gift of breathing, still by grace unfolding in me, is for them as well. At a fundamental level, it ties us all together. The world is closely in the backdrop as I sit down on my prayer mat these days and endeavor to *Make Strong*. Indeed, not an easy thing.

One final, totally Gurdjieffian, prophetic twist: At the end of that same chapter on Hypnotism (Ibid., 522–23) he notes that the invitation to transform these higher cosmic substances embedded in the air is not only a sacred opportunity but also a *collective human obligation*; failure to do so throws the whole system of inter-realmic reciprocal feeding off-kilter. The untransformed "crystallizations" of these higher cosmic substances reign back down on the earth—as viruses! He suggests that it was precisely this imbalance that gave rise to the first global pandemic, the Spanish influenza of 2018! You can dismiss this as poppycock if you like, but at root I believe the old sage may have a point. Our postmodern arrogance and skepticism notwithstanding, we humans are indeed very small cogs in a huge and merciful intercosmic wheel. As we reawaken reverence and gratitude, courage and strength will surely follow.

EXERCISE FOUR:

The Atmosphere Exercise

—Azize, pages 194–96

THE ATMOSPHERE EXERCISE

On August 3, 1944, responding to a woman who said, "My decision is automatic. I do not succeed in feeling like a human being," Gurdjieff said:

1. You must do an exercise to be more collected. Learn to collect yourself. Choose a good moment that seems propitious. Sit down. Let nobody disturb you. Relax yourself. All your attention—all your will is concentrated on your relaxation. You quieten your associations. After—only after, you begin to think.

2. . . . After, when you have quietened your associations, only then, begin the exercise—consciously, with all your attention, all your faculties.

3. You represent to yourself that you are surrounded by an atmosphere. Like the earth, man also has an atmosphere, which surrounds him on all sides, for a meter, more or less—to a limit.

4. In the atmosphere the associations, in ordinary life the thoughts—produce waves. It concentrates at certain places—it recedes; it has movements according to the

direction which you impart to it. This depends on the movement of your thought. Your atmosphere is displaced in the direction in which your thought goes. If you think of your mother who is far away, your atmosphere moves towards the place where your mother is.

5. When you do this exercise, you represent to yourself that this atmosphere has limits. For example, one meter and half, shall we say.

6. Then you concentrate all your attention on preventing your atmosphere from escaping beyond the limit. You do not allow it to go further than one meter or one meter and a half. When you feel your atmosphere quietened, without waves, without movement, then with all your will you suck it into yourself—you conserve yourself in this atmosphere. You draw it consciously into yourself. The more you can, the better it is. To start with it is very tiring.

7. That is how you must do the exercise. Afterwards you rest yourself—you send the exercise to the devil. Repeat it afresh in the evening. This exercise is done especially to allow one to have a collected state.

8. It is the first exercise. It is difficult to penetrate into yourself at the first effort. One must compel the atmosphere to remain within its limits—not allow it to go further than it should. It is the first exercise in order to have a collected state. This exercise I have given to everybody.

9. . . . When you have succeeded in doing that, you will be able to have a truly good state, and you will be able, by your will—to re-enter completely into yourselves.

10. When you say "I am" you will sense that you are in yourself, you will sense in the whole of the body—the

echo of "I"—and when you say "am" you will have the
sensation, completely, that you are you.

11. But if you do it for ten years "I am—I am—I am" it
will lead you to nothing but to be a candidate for the
madhouse. Do that or nothing. Begin everything again
with that exercise. It is the first exercise for remembering oneself.

COMMENTARY

1. "Keep Within"

Keep within. And when they say,
"Look here or look there is Christ, go not forth …"
—Quaker plainsong hymn

This beautiful gem of Quaker wisdom, set to music by Paulette
Meier and well loved by many of you around the Wisdom network, encapsulates both the method and the deeper intention
of the Atmosphere Exercise. Here we will be actively explor-
ing what it means to "keep within": not merely as a spiritual
demeanor, but as an actual mode of embodied presence.

Call it your *aura*, call it the *electromagnetic field of your heart*;
the words all point to the same underlying recognition that "we"
do not end at the outer edge of our skins. We move within an
encompassing energetic field which we ourselves generate, and
which—according to Gurdjieff—we are responsible for maintaining in good working order (i.e., nonfrenetic, contained, and
under our conscious supervision). He picturesquely refers to
this field as our "atmosphere."

Contemplative Christianity has also long prized this state
of inner containment, which is known in the Christian West

as "recollection" and in the Christian East as "vigilance." It is a state of alert, calm, gathered presence. In its absence, the energy around our being rushes and swirls in an automatic jumble, losing much of its directional force while at the same time negatively entangling itself with other similarly untended atmospheres. The result is an energetic cacophony.

This relatively straightforward exercise will help you to begin to settle down within your own atmosphere, keeping your being-energy contained and quiet under your conscious tending.

As usual, the chief culprit is thinking—or, to be more specific, the completely mechanical and autonomous movement of thinking when we are not consciously present. Gurdjieff says arrestingly; "Your atmosphere is displaced in the direction in which your thought moves. If you think of your mother who is far away, your atmosphere moves toward the place where your mother is." To be sure, this speaks of the wondrous, space-traveling capacities of our creative imagination carried on the wings of our attention, *so long as both are under our conscious control.* But when imagination becomes infected with nostalgia or fantasy, or suddenly intoxicated by its own magical powers, then the journey is aborted, and our space traveler falls back under the sway of delusion.

But until you have learned to sense your atmosphere directly, you won't be able to taste the difference between imagination indentured to fantasy and "the real deal." It is a tragic *trompe l'oeil* on which many sincere aspirations have foundered.

In this exercise we practice remaining within our atmosphere, *not letting our thoughts and emotions go ricocheting out beyond the meter to meter-and-a-half circle we imaginatively draw around ourselves.* It is the exact inner equivalent of the task we took on one day during our Wisdom School in the desert near

Tucson: to draw a six-foot ring around ourselves and sit within it for an hour. We are drawing that same ring—only now in the air, not on the ground. This will be the paddock where we contain the wild horse of our thoughts, emotions, and impulses until the whole thing comes quietly into a wordless equanimity.

2. The Gentle Art of Representing

In this exercise we meet for the first time Gurdjieff's unique use of the phrase "represent to yourself" (#5). *Representing to yourself* is not the same thing as *visualizing*. Close, but not the identical. They have subtly different flavors, since they are in fact the work of different centers. Visualizing draws primarily on the intellectual center. Representing remains much closer to sensation. With your attention firmly anchored in your solar plexus (at least that's how it works for me), you simply allow the radius of your attention to expand outward to establish a direct sensate contact with the entire sphere of that atmosphere. You will discover that you are able to do this fairly easily if you don't interfere with the process by thinking.

You may watch how the waves of thinking, emotion, agitation wash across the still waters of your atmosphere. But if you simply "keep within," not allowing yourself to be dragged outside the sphere of your atmosphere, things will quiet down once again, and the depths of a deeper, mysterious aliveness will begin to emerge.

One must also "compel the atmosphere to stay within its limits—not allow it to go further than it can sustain" (#8). That limit is concretely set at a meter to a meter-and-a-half. It actually exists—a palpable energy field. Anything beyond this, and you will likely be venturing out under the sway of thought, emotion, or unanchored visualization. And you will inevitably get tangled up in other people's atmospheres.

I have often used this "sanctuary" of my atmosphere to navigate through a rough patch when a group I am teaching begins to get energetically disturbed (i.e., heady, confrontational, or intoxicated with a kind of group musk). Sometimes the only thing that can be done is to plant my attention in my solar plexus, "shelter in place" within my atmosphere, and hold the space until the disturbed waves subside. Mysteriously, this will often have a calming presence on the whole group. I have learned through repeated hard knocks that this is usually the *only* way to shift the energy. Taking the bait when an inflamed emotional or intellectual challenge has been hurled onto the floor is like pouring gasoline on a fire. Only by standing firm in that stillness will the disturbed atmosphere within the group begin to settle.

And this stands to reason, since the disturbance has been created in the first place by the group leader failing to notice when—carried away by thought, emotion, or passion—the group members have been drawn out of their individual atmospheres. The result will always be trouble.

Learning to stay within one's own atmosphere is not only responsible self-maintenance; it is also foundational group hygiene. We will see more why this is so when we come to the next exercise, The Web.

3. Expanded Attention

There is a very good reason, I believe, that Gurdjieff set the boundary of our personal atmosphere at a meter to a meter-and-a-half; that is the maximum radius that most people, without specialized training, can actually embrace *through direct sensation*, rather than defaulting to visualization. In other words, it is the functional radius of our attention.

I must confess that I have always struggled with the Work phrase, "divided attention," and (whether in the movements, the exercises, or in practical work) its companion instruction: "divide your attention." I know this instruction comes with hoary authority—Gurdjieff himself taught it. So it is with justifiable fear and trembling that I raise my dissenting voice here—may God smite me if I am wrong! But I stand by my own experience: *attention cannot be divided.* Like the body of Christ in Symeon the New Theologian's celebrated poem, it is "indivisibly whole, seamless in [its] Godhood." And since it is thus by nature infinite, it cannot be divided by any finite integer. You cannot place half your attention on your right arm and half on "I AM." The two must occur simultaneously, held together in a three-dimensional space—a sphere of attention with its center located deeper within.

"Where do you pay attention *from*?" Ben Grant asked us almost offhandedly at the end of a teaching session with the Toronto group in the early 1990s. Ben Grant was an elder in the Work, a first-generation student of Gurdjieff, by then well into his eighties.

The question riveted me. In all my years in the Work I had never heard it asked either before or since. But the answer from within was not long in coming. Nor has it ever varied.

The seat of my attention is in my solar plexus.

With my attention firmly grounded there (which is also, in many chakra systems, the seat of the personal will), I then project it out like a light-beam, scribing a sphere according to the radius—to the candlepower—of my attention.

Within that three-dimensional space, attention is not divided; rather, it expands effortlessly to fill the space, just like air in a balloon when you blow it up. Everything within the radius of that sphere can be *simultaneously* comprehended, held in balance, like planets circling around a sun. When I am on the movements floor, for example, I do not apportion 30 percent of my attention to my feet, 30 percent to the arms, and 30 percent to the counting task; in that mentalized configuration my attention swiftly collapses. Rather, fiercely gathered and present at the seat of my attention ("quivering like a drop of mercury," in Rumi's evocative phrase) I simply *do*—for as far out as my attention can hold the unbroken field.

That is the beauty of the Atmosphere Exercise as Gurdjieff offers it to us here. Our "atmosphere" is really the functional circumference of our attention; within it, we get to taste ourselves directly. It is as close as we can get to touching our own essence. As close as we get to a direct, sensation of our being, our "Real I." Within this cloistered garden the fragrance is sweet. It is nurturing. No wonder Gurdjieff encourages us to suck it in.

Go much beyond that meter-and-a-half and the attention buckles; you collapse back into the *story* of yourself, the emotions, the vicarious projections. Back to viewing yourself through the periscope of your mind. That is why Gurdjieff was so insistent on "compelling the atmosphere to remain within its limits." Better to stay with a small truth than a large illusion.

In any group activity, *your foremost priority is to take responsibility for maintaining the unity and coherence of your own atmosphere.* As the old Shaker maxim goes, "We should pass by each other lightly, like angels." When we get pulled off-balance out of three-centered awareness—when we get co-opted by our agendas, our emotions, the excitement racing through the crowd—then the external manifestations emerging from our disturbed atmosphere will always be cacophonous. They will always clash with and incite other atmospheres. Agitation, posturing, headiness, stridency, sentimentality, emotional manipulation are always the results that are initially perceptible in the raised decibels and sharper tone of voices and in general body agitation—once you've trained yourself to look. This is how groups get shanghaied, and sincerely intended visions and aspirations go down in flames.

I repeat: in all groups, but particularly in spiritual groups, the responsible custody of your atmosphere is your first and primary obligation. As the individual atmospheres go, so will the group atmosphere as well. If something is going off-track energetically—*STOP!* Put the argument on pause and attend to this beautiful, simple exercise to restore and recollect your own atmosphere. Then you can all begin in a better place and carry on with the cosmic work that a "seamless and indivisible" group atmosphere can contribute so profoundly to our aching and fractured planet.

As usual, Rumi nails it. Here is the rest of the poem, "The Waterwheel":

> Stay together, friends.
> Don't scatter and sleep.
>
> Our friendship is made
> of being awake.
>
> The waterwheel accepts water
> and turns and gives it away,
> weeping.
>
> That way it stays in the garden,
> whereas another roundness rolls
> through a dry riverbed looking
> for what it thinks it wants.
>
> Stay here, quivering with each moment
> like a drop of mercury.

The Web Exercise

—Azize, pages 200–202

THE WEB EXERCISE

This exercise is unique in the Gurdjieff repertoire in that it requires the members of a group to work at it in conjunction with each other, both when they had come together as a group and while they went about their usual activities. It hails from the transcript of May 25, 1944, when Gurdjieff said:

> It is possible to have a common contact through the aim. It is possible with practice. For example, when you are seated together do not spend your time internally like in life. Use this occasion to do an exercise; suggest to yourself that this atmosphere about you, wakes up to the desire to go towards the aim . . . everybody here. This atmosphere is warming for an aspiring with all your being towards a common aim. When you find yourselves together, suddenly, automatically it produces this heating. You can have a reciprocal action on a whole city. Paris is big; but if you begin it will become, little by little, possible that, if one movement

is produced in a corner of this atmosphere, it will start an unrest which will spread overall.

You have knowledge of different telepathic acts. It is as if the atmosphere became large; a material is formed like the web of a spider. If, in one of the meshes, a new force enters, this can correspond in the whole network, like in an electric conduit. . . . You create a factor of inclination for succeeding in your aim with all your mass. For this it is necessary that two things happen, auto-suggestion and representation by forms, but subjective forms. In the beginning you will understand what is happening; it is not important to picture it to oneself exactly. Imagine that in you there is a network. If one current comes in one point, it shall arrive everywhere, if one sensation of warmth is in one point, all the points shall feel the heat, the cold. Picture how what happens in one place happens everywhere.

After some further exchange, Gurdjieff instructed them:

Try now to do this exercise of forming a web. The whole brotherhood also did the same thing. You know the proverb: "one for all, all for one." In ordinary life, this is a lie, because it is not realizable. But here is a brotherhood. They all have one common aim. One of them is there; but he must desire that all attain it, and inversely, the others are also obliged to help him. . . . There exist two things; matter and force. This exercise is to urge, to excite, to animate.

COMMENTARY

1. Preliminary Remarks on the Web Exercise

I had not originally planned to include this exercise in this introductory sampling and still have serious misgivings about sharing it now. There's a significant risk that some of you may be tempted to try it out under inappropriate conditions and wind up in a hall of mirrors.

But the exercise so clearly furnishes the bridge, both conceptually and practically, between the Atmosphere Exercise we have just been working with and the magisterial Four Ideals Exercise upon which we are about to embark, that to leave it off the table turns out to be impossible. You will meet a new side of Gurdjieff here, a whole new depth to his collective and compassionate engagement with the world that few commentators, even those senior in the Work, have sufficiently noticed.

So, here's the *caveat* up front: Please do not try out this exercise with your newfound friends in your online spiritual study group. Repeat: *DO NOT!* It needs to be anchored in actual on-the-ground experience, lived cheek-to-jowl with your fellow seekers, shored up by a hefty component of practical physical work. Full engagement of the moving center is mandatory for understanding, for as in the Rule of Saint Benedict, it is the intentional, rhythmic circulation through a daily round of activities—prayer alone, prayer together, work alone, work together—that undergirds the gradual transfiguration of understanding. If you try to do this with your virtual group, you will be starting too far up in your body and in only one quadrant of activity. You will inevitably mistake the emotional feeling of closeness with your group members for the imperishably finer, more spacious, more impartial substance that enters "from above … when the conditions are right."

Instead, I would ask you to try to recall a time in your actual on-the-ground group experience when something of this other order of intensity entered. A whole different flavor, a whole different taste from either clinging, sentimentality, or enthusiasm. *Represent* it to yourself; use your conscious imagination to actually *make it present to yourself* again.

I can recall two such experiences clearly marked by this other quality of fineness. The first was during a Wisdom School several years ago on the Olympic Peninsula, where our combined Fourth Way/contemplative group suddenly found itself in the midst of a morning of *sohbet* (spiritual conversation and dialogue) thinking as if with one intelligence, seamlessly articulating a whole that was infinitely more than the sum of its parts. Quakers point toward this same experience when they speak of a "gathered" or "covered" meeting. In the utter stillness of their melded atmospheres something of a different substantiality sometimes enters in.

The other experience was more recent; at our Gurdjieff/ Teilhard seminar at Claymont just last fall, where the gathered meeting actually went on for several days across a variety of spheres of activity. Maybe it had something to do with our opening-night Eucharist on the movements floor, commemorating the seventieth anniversary of Gurdjieff's passing. Maybe it was our daily work with the Make Strong Exercise. Maybe it was the movements themselves; they have an uncanny capacity to evoke this dimension. Whatever the combination, the group soon fell into an effortless collective transfiguration. It cut across the teaching, the practical work, the work in movements. We were effortlessly carried as if on a wing. We saw things, understood things during that liminal week that simply cannot be reconstructed now. But we knew it was food from above.

And we are still drawing on it now.

I share these personal recollections to help you get a taste of the *quality of oneness* we will be looking for as we begin in the next post to ponder the remarkable assertions Gurdjieff is making in his Web Exercise. Using Fourth Way language, one might say it bears the distinct fragrance of "higher emotional center" and even "higher intellectual center." It cannot—repeat—*cannot* be generated from below, from even the most fervent application of our usual wishing, desiring, aiming. Instead, you must wait in stillness, quietly poised within your own atmosphere, attending with bare simplicity to the next thing that needs to be done until, in the words of Paulette Meier's beautiful Quaker chant, "light arises out of darkness and leads thee."

Then and only then are you really clear to participate in forming that web which does indeed have the capacity to significantly shift the state of things both in our own world and in worlds beyond.

2. The Group Atmosphere

Just as there is an individual atmosphere, so there is also a group atmosphere, formed from the aggregation of individual atmospheres. Gurdjieff picturesquely calls it a web. When this web is clear and conscious, it can become a tremendous source of support and transformation, both for its individual group members and for larger planetary purposes.

Gurdjieff may never have heard those contemporary buzzwords: "quantum entanglement" and "non-localized action," but in this exercise (which in my opinion is less an exercise than an extended reflection) he demonstrates a precocious awareness of both these dimensions of nonlinear causality. In this exercise he sets before us the dazzling possibility that *a group which has become capable of navigating consciously in these deeper waters can become a profound force for good.*

Don't pass through the metaphor of the web too quickly, taking it simply as a synonym for a network. When you look closely, you will see that Gurdjieff is actually talking about a *substance* ("a material," as he calls it) manifested in and through that web that actually creates the web in the first place. It's this substance we want to keep our eyes on. I have tried to call your attention to it in a few of my earlier posts.

The substance in question is this mysterious quality of "fineness"—of a higher order of synergy, understanding, clarity—that sometimes flows through a group and lifts it into a whole new realm of expressivity, as if the group is with one body and soul collectively "in the flow." We experience it usually as "oneness" and tend to process it as a *feeling*. What is actually going on, however, is that we are collectively tasting a substance of an infinitely more delicate, crystalline nature, a substance perhaps bearing the fragrance of that "sacred *aiëssakhladonn*" I referred to in my commentary on the Make Strong Exercise—that direct nurturance emanating from our Most Holy Sun Absolute. It takes a prepared heart and a prepared nervous system to be able to partake directly of food of this subtlety. This is true both for the individual and for the group. But when that preparation has been carefully made, miracles can happen.

The quantum entanglement extends in two directions: between the group and its individual members, and between the group atmosphere and the planetary atmosphere. In this and the next post I will be focusing on the first of these aspects, then I will turn to Gurdjieff's astounding assertion that through the warming produced within the web *"you can have a reciprocal action on a whole city."*

THE CONSCIOUS WORK GROUP

We're not talking about *any* old group here, of course. By "group" (or "brotherhood," as he also calls it here) Gurdjieff means *an intentional work group* bound together by a common aim and a willingness to abide by the protocols of conscious labor and intentional suffering. If the atmosphere of the group is clear and consciously tended, and if the desire to "go towards the aim" (as Gurdjieff puts it) is strong enough, then the group can accomplish collectively—through its melded atmosphere—a transformation unavailable to an individual working alone.

The stipulations are clear, however. The first is that the group must be held together *at the apex* (in Azize's perceptive comment) by their "shared conscious aim." Held together from their Omega Point, as Teilhard might say. No lesser motivation will do. A conscious work group is not for support, fellowship, or a feeling of belonging. None of these proximate aims, no matter how laudable in their own right, are strong enough to endure the ravages when the shadow side starts to surface. Only the true north of the common aim will guide the seekers across the darkened waters.

The second stipulation is that this brotherhood must truly be "one for all, all for one." The terms for arriving at the destination are that *all arrive together*; all are bound in a covenant of mutual becoming. This is a core theme for Gurdjieff. You will also see it resonating very strongly as well in his fifth Obligolnian striving: "the striving always to assist the most rapid perfecting of other beings, both those similar to oneself and those of other forms, up to the degree of the sacred '*Martfotai*,' that is, up to the degree of self-individuality." (Gurdjieff, 352).

It is to my mind no coincidence that exactly these same two stipulations form the twin pillars of the Rule of Saint Benedict, which has guided Christian seekers for some fifteen hundred years now, the longest continuously surviving conscious fellowship in the Christian West. The sense of a common aim in this "school for the Lord's service" pervades the entire Rule. Perhaps less well known is the sublime reflection in Chapter 72 (the next-to-the-last) on "The Good Zeal of Monks":

> This, then, is the good zeal that monks must foster
> with fervent love: They should try to be the first to
> show respect to the other, supporting with the greatest
> patience one another's weaknesses of body or behavior
> and earnestly competing in obedience to one another.
> No one is to pursue what he judges better for himself,
> but instead, what he judges better for someone else.

It's also much the same, incidentally, in a good choir—which in my own experience has actually been the closest approximation of the ideal Gurdjieff is laying before us here (though of course with a more limited aim). No good choir forms to offer fellowship to its members. The choristers are there for one purpose only: to collectively serve the music, give it voice, and unlock its beauty. Everybody yearns to feast on this beauty, and they can only recognize their aim collectively. Sometimes, choir members do not like each other; they wince at each other's mannerisms and bear each other's infirmities through gritted teeth. But in order to make the music happen, they must defer to each other and "earnestly compete in obedience to one another." A choir of individual prima donnas will never deliver the music. They cannot form a coherent atmosphere.

What can be accomplished when a group atmosphere is woven on the loom of these two great stipulations? Plenty. We'll consider some of the practical implications in my next post.

3. Yin and Yang

PHASE ONE: THE YANG

The Web Exercise is unique in the Gurdjieff repertoire, Azize comments, "in that it requires the members of the group to work at it in conjunction with each other, both when they come together as a group and while they go about their usual [i.e., separated] activities." The exercise thus has a kind of "yin and yang" quality to it, and it is in coming to see how these two phases work together that the real learning is to be had.

I don't want to push the yin/yang metaphor too far, but let's say that the *yang* phase corresponds to the time when the group is actually physically working together. Here Gurdjieff suggests that rather than just "disappearing" into one's private inner work (as happens all too often in spiritual groups), a deliberate effort be made to reach out and establish a direct contact with that common aim that has brought the members together in the first place.

"Direct contact," of course, means through *sensing*. In the same way we have already practiced sensing our leg, sensing our head, sensing our atmosphere—we now simply expand the radius of our attention one notch farther and *directly sense the atmosphere of the entire group*, the atmosphere called into being by the confluence of all those individual aims.

In so doing, a mutual quickening happens. The group atmosphere is consciously activated and synchronized; it comes into coherence and becomes a unified field. As Gurdjieff picturesquely puts it, "The atmosphere is warming for an aspiring with all your being towards a common aim." Then, from the warmth of that activated field, all members can individually draw reinforcement as they work together toward the fulfillment of that common aim. This is the "fineness" I spoke of earlier, the mysterious "something" that sometimes enters and allows a group to work miles above their own heads in a seemingly effortless clarity. I believe it is actually *an emergent property of the whole*, of the group atmosphere that has been summoned into life.

I repeat here my earlier caveat that the real benefit conferred through an on-the-ground group is that it ensures the balanced participation of all three centers. As the group circulates through its rota of daily activities—teaching, exercises, practical work, movements, meditation—the sensation of unity gradually grows across a spectrum of activities and becomes deeply seated in the body as *a felt-sense memory*, not simply an emotion of closeness or a speculative ideal. In that deeply embodied configuration, it can be more quickly drawn on when the group enters Phase Two.

PHASE TWO: THE YIN

Once that morphogenetic field has been created, the first surprise in store for the individual members is the discovery that *the group atmosphere does not disperse when the group itself physically disperses*. The atmosphere remains in place, continuing to infuse and bind its members together ("at the apex") even though they may be widely scattered geographically. The product of a higher order of causality, it is not limited by the conventions of space and time. Its operational mode is *non-localized action*. Azize comments: "Movement is effectively instantaneous in time and space, for conscious activity is realized in higher dimensions" (Azize, 201). There is no need for members to be physically (or even virtually) in contact with each other; what is known in one corner of the web is mysteriously available throughout the entire web. Encouragement, insight, solidarity, healing, prophetic initiative, the sudden entry of third force—all of these are knowable and instantly available to all within the "warmed atmosphere" and sheltering intelligence of the web.

Learning how to work with this property comprises the *yin* phase of this exercise.

As you can now more fully imagine, this is the main reason I have been reluctant to jump whole-hog onto the bandwagon of simply riding out the pandemic with a proliferation of Zoom groups, online study groups, Zoom retreats, even Zoom liturgies. First of all, it isn't a priority, *or in fact even necessary*, in an authentic wisdom group. Everything you need is there already through the common sustenance flowing to you through the web. Second, this continued allure of the surface pulls you away from the level at which the real juice is flowing, the level at which you have by grace and grit been preparing yourself to work. It substitutes a more superficial level of "staying in touch" and horizontal fellowship for the alchemical fusion of souls that is awaiting you at the depths. A bit like trying to grope your way in the dark with the help of a flashlight when what you really need is to learn how to see in the dark.

The first step is the hardest. Lean into the emptiness! Don't immediately rush to fill up all the available space. Lean into the darkness and let your eyes adjust. Little by little you'll discover that you're actually seeing a new landscape, seeing in a slightly different way. The deeper clues of connectedness begin to fill in for you, announcing their presence in small and often surprising ways. As your imaginal vision gains strength, that strength flows back into the web, and the web itself gains strength and presence—presence enough, eventually, to begin to hold healing and even prophetic force within its collective atmosphere.

And yes, I know. Some of you are holding teaching and pastoral posts with commitments that must be upheld and with folks out there who are frightened, lonely, and disrupted, longing for connection at any level. Do your work; feed the hungry. But when you are finished with what you have been given to do this day, shut down the computer and lean into the emptiness; the atmosphere has your back! Trust that what we have built on the ground over these past two decades during our *yang* phase of our Wisdom work, is now there for us all as we collectively enter the *yin* phase, which may feel like a diminishment but in fact "draws the circle just."

4. Global Warming Revisited

The far more interesting possibilities implicit in this exercise, however, open up for me in the opposite direction: between the group atmosphere and the planetary atmosphere. Let's say that a conscious work group has managed to establish a group atmosphere that is coherent, stable, and clear. Can this atmosphere then interact with our larger planetary atmosphere to actually bring a new influence into the situation? Can it really indeed "have a reciprocal action on a whole city"?

Gurdieff's answer—offered allusively but fervently—is that *it can indeed*. And if this is the case, it opens before our Wisdom sangha a powerful new avenue of service, together with a very stringent road to tow if we are to make good on it.

Azize makes the invitation explicit in his lean, four-bullet-point commentary:

> "Second," says Gurdjieff, "when the people whose atmosphere form the web come together with a common aim, there is a warming in the web. This invisible reality is not something neutral: It is positive. It also

means that a conscious aim, especially perhaps a common conscious aim, is an active element not only in a group but even for society, represented here by the city of Paris."

While Paris may indeed be intended only to "represent" the larger society, I think it's important not to lose sight of the particular context here. Azize notes the date of this exercise as May 25, 1944—or in other words, less than two weeks before the allied forces will arrive on Normandy Beach and begin their relentless drive east. Three months to the day later, Paris will be free, and the former "Fête St. Louis" will have been rebaptised as "La Fête de la Liberation."

Throughout the entire dark and terrible four years of the occupation, Gurdjieff had held his ground right there in Paris. Unlike most other spiritual teachers of his era, who had fled to places of greater tranquility to carry on their spiritual work undisturbed, Gurdjieff had stayed put, finding the conditions for transformation not in tranquility but in fierce presence. From his small apartment less than a mile as the crow flies from the Nazi command post on the Place de la Concorde, he simply went about feeding people, spiritually and literally. Drawing on his proverbial skills as a magician and wheeler-dealer, he somehow managed to acquire valuable stockpiles of staples and even gourmet items. The staples he stored in a back pantry, accessible through a back stairwell that was never locked. The gourmet fare he laid out in lavish banquets before whatever assortment of pilgrims happened to assemble at the table that night. There was teaching, inquiry, liberally flowing Armagnac—and a suffusion of love that still blazes in the hearts and writings of those students blessed enough to sit at his feet during those times. His teaching became simpler, more direct, more overtly religious, more compassionate and universal in its focus. He was literally warming the atmosphere of Paris.

Some of you may know of the white-knuckle drama unfolding at the same time (grippingly recorded in the book *Is Paris Burning?*). Recognizing that the German retreat was inevitable, Hitler had laid in place an elaborate scheme to leave as much damage in his wake as he could. Bombs had been laid beneath the celebrated monuments of Notre Dame and the Louvre. All was in readiness for the obliteration of a thousand years of Western cultural history. The only thing still awaiting was the command from the German commanding officer, Dietrich von Choltitz, poised there on the Place de la Concorde.

Somehow that command never came. Like a tide that reaches its flood and then noiselessly recedes, so the German army of the occupation simply receded. No decision was ever made *not* to bomb Paris; the moment simply slipped away. No one knows exactly why. That is the sort of thing that can happen when an atmosphere is warmed.

In linear causality, of course, there is absolutely no way of proving a connection between these events. In imaginal causality (that higher dimension Azize referred to where conscious work takes place) there is no way of *not* seeing it; the lines of causality cross vividly before your eyes— in the web.

I am not saying that Gurdjieff deliberately set out to accomplish that result; almost certainly he did not. It never works that tightly. He simply felt in his great heart the atmosphere of a Paris grown brittle and mineral under the occupying forces and undertook to supply the missing element. Call it food, call it abundance, call it love; without it the human spirit starves and life grows frozen and intractable. When the atmosphere thaws, when even in one tiny corner of it life becomes flowing and supple, then something new is possible everywhere. For as Gurdjieff pointedly observes, "If one current comes in at one point, it shall arrive everywhere, if one sensation of warmth is in one point, all the points shall feel the heat. Picture how what happens in one place happens everywhere."

I lay this story before your creative imagination to invite the Wisdom Community to envision a broader and bolder way that we might intentionally work in the world. A web is underutilized if we only use it to shore up our personal sense of safety and connectedness within our immediate group. It can more powerfully be used to offer *direct transfusions* of hope, courage, compassion, and resilience to an entire planet grown dark and mineral for want of these things. It can begin to warm the atmosphere in the inner ground, so that new movement in the outer ground becomes possible.

There are cautions and protocols around this kind of work, essentially encapsulated in the classic monastic vows of "chastity, poverty, and obedience." I will be looking at these in my next post. But for now, let's stay with the extraordinarily high possibility being laid before us here: that a "warmed atmosphere" constellated within a group through the melding of their common aim *can then be turned outward,* where it can indeed have a reciprocal action on a whole city. Even a whole world.

5. Chastity, Poverty, and Obedience

You might picture Gurdjieff's web as a two-directional amplifier. Directed inwardly, it enables individual group members to draw continuing replenishment from the collective strength of the whole. Directed outwardly, it boosts the magnitude of the group's common aim to a point where "you can have a reciprocal action on a whole city." Through the amplifying effect of its web, the group becomes a real player in the planetary atmosphere.

This is an awesome invitation, of course. Were our hearts not burning to hear it? But it is also "awesome" in the traditional sense of the word, meaning *needing to be approached with due humility and awe.* For it carries a solemn responsibility and comes with all-too-real risks of running off the rails. Particularly for us "newbies" who have not been fully prepared to work at this level, and surrounded as we are by a culture that has largely forgotten this level even exists, the dangers are all too real of getting shanghaied by lesser agendas. Powerful work can indeed be done here—and I think is in fact crying out to be done here—but some fairly rigorous protocols need to be observed in order to ensure that our work remains sober, lucid, and safe.

As I mentioned in my last post, most of the rubrics are already embedded in those classic monastic vows of chastity, poverty, and obedience—once you learn to hear these not as ascetic renunciations but as practical safeguards for all esoteric work.

CHASTITY, in this case means: "Keep your atmosphere within its atmosphere."

In the Atmosphere Exercise you practiced on an individual basis keeping your atmosphere within a certain finite limit (a meter to a meter-and-a-half): not letting it escape beyond that limit, not letting it get distended by thought or emotional waves. You practiced sitting within it, allowing its waves to quiet and learning to maintain conscious stewardship of it as you brought it with you into your daily rounds. The same is true, on a larger scale, of your group atmosphere. It needs to stay coherent and clear, able to stretch across whatever distance it circumscribes, without being unduly ruffled by waves of passion or grandiosity. It wants to be a still pond in which the full moon is reflected. All urgency or self-importance will immediately kill this reflective capacity—and alas, those impulses can ignite like brushfire in an atmosphere gathered around a common aim. Considerable restraint is needed here—*chastity*—to keep from being taken over by what Gurdjieff rightly calls "a misuse of the sex center" (i.e., intoxication, over-excitement, demagoguery, and all too often, violence).

POVERTY means: "Give up all attachment to outcome. Even all curiosity about outcome."

It's a natural human inclination to want to hold our aim a little too tightly and then wait eagerly for the results. We light a candle and visualize a specific outcome: the healing of our planet, the disappearance of the corona virus, a restoration of the broken links of our human community. But it never works this linearly and in fact can't work this linearly, for *imaginal causality is not linear but synchronous*. It produces its effects non-locally, instantaneously, in places you'd never expect or with partners you don't even know you're playing with. Perhaps the atmosphere of your group melds with a compatible atmosphere of, say, some Sufi dervishes in Central Asia you don't even know are out there. And in a manger in Bethlehem, a Messiah is quietly born. It's like that—way more indirect, way more playful. You simply carry your little pebble of conscious striving to the edge of the cliff and toss it into the ocean. The rest is in the hands of God.

And yes, there are certain initiated elders who do in fact have the authority to bend intention to a desired end. Fortunately, this power lies beyond most of us—for good reason—and one does well to tread with utmost humility here. Creative imagination fettered to a still untamed ego will always result in some variation of magic—at best, merely overwrought and foolish, at worst, deadly dangerous.

OBEDIENCE means: *Listen, Listen, Listen!*

In fact, that's literally true. Obedience comes from the Latin *ob-audire*, which means "listen to the depths," or "listen *from* the depths." Ninety percent of the work you will be doing inside your group web is listening: listening to one another, listening to the subtle directives that emerge out of the depths as you gain more proficiency in attuning to them, listening to the needs that the rapidly changing conditions in the outer world are laying before you.

The operative model here is actually best captured in that relatively new physics buzzword, a "self-specifying system," of which the cell is our baseline example. The cell demonstrates diversity of function within an overall unity, maintained by an instantaneous capacity for self-regulation governed by its DNA and RNA. Inside the cell there is always a dance going on, a continuous process of listening, of making microadjustments. Through that dance the cell remains in dynamic equilibrium (i.e., *alive*).

The wonderful implication here—fully glimpsed though not fully articulated by Gurdjieff—is that the group web is in fact a self-specifying system. It has "emergent properties"— capabilities not present in its individual components but vested collectively in the whole. (That is again that mysterious *fineness* we've spoken about several times before.) Individual members sacrifice a degree of personal autonomy in order to partake of the far greater capacities of the whole. Through *listening*—that continuous dance of adjusting, deferring—those capacities become available to each member insofar as he or she remains in coherence with the whole. The web remains *alive*.

In the end, one either surrenders to this higher level of wholeness or one does not. What *doesn't* work is to sit on the fence.

Modern buzzword or not, the idea itself has been around for a long time. Saint Paul was already onto it in the first century with his celebrated teaching, "We are all members of the one body of Christ." And so, it comes as no surprise, perhaps, that these ancient vows should again demonstrate their timeless timeliness as we now scramble to self-organize at a new evolutionary level in order to meet the evolutionary challenge.

The Four Ideals Exercise

—Azize, pages 231–40

THE FOUR IDEALS EXERCISE

On October 1, 1948, Gurdjieff taught George Adie the Four Ideals Exercise, a "subjective exercise." Adie worked with this exercise for five months, until some point in March 1949. In this exercise the exercitant attempts to make contact with the four "ideals" (Christ, Buddha, Muhammad, and Lama) and introduce into the exercitant's own body the "higher substances" that are produced when worshippers pray or address themselves to those "ideals."

The exercise reads (incorporating the Adies' corrections and editing, and making insignificant changes to layout and punctuation):

> On earth all people have an ideal which they situate far off in space, high above themselves. Towards this ideal they send their emanations. They pray to it, they stretch towards it, their emanations mount towards it. Their emanations do not all have the same force. Some of them can hardly rise at all, others go further, further

even than the atmosphere of the earth, yet others mount almost to the very ideal.

The emanations on leaving the earth are dispersed, then they mount, further on they collect together to form at a certain level above the atmosphere of the earth a sort of reservoir or foyer of substances.

We represent to ourselves that this foyer of substances is situated midway between the earth and the point of concentration which represents the ideal of the believers. The ideal himself is too far for an unprepared man to be able to enter into contact with him, but the man can, if he tries with determination enter into contact with this foyer of substances formed from the concentration of the vibrations sent by the believers towards their ideal and the man can assimilate these substances and accumulate them in himself. He can do it by establishing through the concentration of his will a connection in the form of a line or thread between this foyer and some part or other of his own body.

The exercise is given to achieve this aim. We choose four ideals: Muhammad, Christ, Buddha, Lama. We represent that their essence exists somewhere in space, in a place situated above the country where they lived:

Muhammad	above Mecca and Medina
Christ	above Jerusalem
Buddha	above India
Lama	above Tibet

In representing to ourselves each of these ideals, the thought goes immediately in the direction in space where the ideal is situated. The exercise consists in establishing a contact between one of the limbs of the body and the foyer of substances formed by the vibrations of the faithful in the direction of the ideal.

For this, each of the four limbs of the body represents one of the four ideals. The right arm represents Muhammad, the left arm Christ, the right leg Buddha, the left leg Lama.

First, establish a contact between the right arm and that part of space in which Muhammad is situated, where are concentrated the vibrations sent by the faithful towards Muhammad. One must suck, attract to oneself; by means of a thread which serves to connect us; the substance concentrated at that place, and with this substance fill the right arm.

Second do the same thing by means of a contact between Buddha and the right leg.

Third the same between Christ and the left arm.

Fourth the same between Lama and the left leg.

At this stage the four limbs are like accumulators fully charged.

Now follows the second part of the exercise:

Breathe in air consciously while drawing into yourself the substances accumulated in the limbs so that it can flow to meet the air which you are breathing in. It mixes with the air by itself, at the level of the breast. Then pour it into the sex organs.

I AM, in two parts.

With "I" feel the sex organs, with "AM" fill up the seven parts of the body one after the other.

1. "I"   feel the sex organs
    "Am"   with the substance accumulated in them
           fill up the right leg by pouring into it this
           substance
2. "I"   feel the sex organs
    "Am"   fill up the left leg
3. "I"   feel the sex organs
    "Am"   fill up the lower part of the abdomen
4. "I"   feel the sex organs
    "Am"   fill up the whole of the abdomen
5. "I"   feel the sex organs
    "Am"   fill up the torso
6. "I"   feel the sex organs
    "Am"   fill up the two arms and the shoulders
7. "I"   fill up the head

Then "I AM" several times. "I" am conscious of
the whole of the body with a feeling centered in the
solar plexus. "AM" again am conscious of the whole
of the body, with a sensation centered in the vertebral
column.

After that, rest ten or fifteen minutes in a collected
state, that is to say, do not allow thought or feeling or
organic instinct to pass outside the limit of the atmosphere of the body. Rest contained so that your nature
can assimilate in calmness the results deposited in you,
which otherwise would be lost in vain.

COMMENTARY

1. Preliminary to the Four Ideals Exercise

The Four Ideals Exercise is complex and demanding. It will draw on all the practices you've been working with in the exercises to date, then up the ante still another notch. Of all the Gurdjieff exercises, it is the most cosmic in scope and the most unabashedly mystical in tone. In the Bennett line of the Work, students were not even allowed to embark on it before spending a year in specifically designed preparatory exercises. While the Bennett version of this exercise is somewhat more technical than the original Gurdjieffian version we'll be considering here, one is nonetheless well advised to approach this exercise in a state of inner preparedness and with all due respect. The terrain we will be traversing here is numinous and powerful.

My purpose in what may have seemed to you all like a lengthy digression on the Web Exercise was really to open up some sense of the vastness of this terrain, both in the enormity of its scale and in the profundity of its demand. The Four Ideals Exercise really unfolds against the backdrop of the entire *Megalocosmos*, as Gurdjieff calls it—that is, embracing the full wingspan of the Ray of Creation in the dance of reciprocal giving and receiving that maintains the entire created order in a dynamic equilibrium. Both horizontal and vertical exchange are fully in play here, and if your heart is strong enough to take it, and your presence deep enough to hold it, you can indeed begin to sense yourself as a living particle of this infinite cosmic dance. You begin to taste the true scale of things—and to grasp, in those immortal words of Saint Paul, "how wide and long and deep and high" is the Mercy flowing through these ancient cosmic ley lines.

This exercise will call specifically on four skills you've learned in our earlier exercises:

a. The four-limb body rotation (Clear Impressions, Lord Have Mercy) together with spinal extension (Clear Impressions);
b. The I AM, placed on the breath (Make Strong);
c. The retention during the outbreath of some finer particulate of "being food" carried in the air (Make Strong);
d. The capacity to "represent" a notion to yourself (Make Strong, Atmosphere, Web).

In addition, you will find it helpful to call upon the following more general capacities—all of them hopefully now well-imprinted through your work with the previous exercises—for the sensation of full, three-centered participation ("With all three centers, do!"):

a. Some feeling for the complementary (i.e., symbiotic unity of I AM and Lord Have Mercy;
b. A visceral sense of what it means to remain within your atmosphere;
c. Some feeling for how individual atmospheres can be joined at the apex to form a web through which energy and assistance flows;
4.
5. A direct sensation of what it means to "free my head. Free it from words" to make it remain in the body.

Before plunging into the Four Ideals Exercise, my recommendation would be that you take some time revisiting each of the earlier exercises, reviewing these individual components with the awareness that they are about to be synthesized in a whole new way. Practice the skills that come hard; luxuriate in the ones that come easily. Prepare yourself both inwardly and outwardly for the task you are about to take on.

And remember, *take your time!* There is no rush to get through these exercises; any impression that this is some sort of an e-course with a curriculum and timeline is simply a trick of the presentational format. In the original circumstances— *still* the normative circumstances within properly constituted Fourth Way groups—students would regularly work for months on a single exercise, each pass-through taking them deeper and deeper into the hidden treasures to be revealed there. A new exercise would be introduced *only as the students were ready* and according to no predetermined order or timeline other than the readiness itself. Many of these exercises were not even originally intended for group use at all; they were "subjective," in Gurdjieff's words, individually created or customized for a specific recipient to meet a specific developmental need. Just as in *lectio divina*, if you rush through it, you've missed the whole point.

Over the next several postings I will share a few comments on the Four Ideals Exercise— intended, as always, only to get you launched. The rest is up to you, your fellow travelers on this journey, and hopefully some assistance flowing to us from those Four Ideals themselves. In any case, the commentaries will be still be there for you on this page for when you are ready, and there is no race course or time clock. Like the Mad Hatter, "how you get there is where you'll arrive."

2. Four Persons, Not Four Principles

The Four Ideals Exercise consists of two parts linked together by a short, crucial bridge. Each of these three segments poses its own challenges, but the first section is literally "the biggest stretch."

In this section you will be doing the familiar limb rotation (though in a slightly unfamiliar order.) But now, in addition to the direct sensing of the limb itself, you will also be attempting to establish a contact between that limb and one of "the four ideals," as Gurdjieff calls them—four sacred individuals who stand at the headwaters of their respective religious lineages and have served this planet with the highest degree of purity and devotion. These are Muhammed (right arm), Buddha (right leg), Christ (left arm), and Lama (left leg).

To be more accurate, you will be trying to establish the contact between your limb and the prayer-rich atmosphere hovering just above the place where each prophet lived: for Muhammed, above Mecca and Medina; for Buddha, above India; for Christ, above Jerusalem; for Lama, above Tibet. In the Adie version of the exercise (which here, as usual, forms the basis for Azize's commentary) this atmosphere is depicted as the "foyer of substances" where the cumulative energy of the prayers, aspiration, and devotion of the faithful are concentrated. The invitation here is to establish a connection—a thread — between each of these foyers and the corresponding body part, and through that thread begin to "assimilate these substances and accumulate them in yourself"—presumably for the building up of your own higher being-bodies (Azize, 231).

If you feel your head starting to spin here, it's understandable. There is enough audaciousness, challenge, and plain old *huh?* packed into just those two sentences to keep me going on these commentaries if I wanted to for several months yet. But if we take it in small bites and limit ourselves only to the most important points, I hope you will be able to stay aboard this exercise long enough to at least get a glimpse of where it's heading.

So, starting at the top: First of all, these "four ideals" are not ideals in the sense that we now typically understand this word. They are not values, virtues, or noble ideas you want to emulate in your life. They are *actual embodied individuals*, who physically walked on this planet and carried us all on their backs. In the Bennett version of this exercise, they are known as "the Four Prophets," but to my (Christian) theologically trained ears, "prophets" sets the bar a little too low. Prophets come from below; sacred individuals come from above. Whether you call them avatars, "Messengers from Above," or "the Highest and Most Saintly Common Cosmic Sacred Individuals" (Gurdjieff, 317), in reference to the very Saintly Ashiata Shiemash), the point is that these "four ideals" are human beings of the highest order of spiritual magnitude. They emanate from realms far higher than our own along the Ray of Creation, and bear the luminous substantiality of those realms even as they walk about in human flesh.

So I had to chuckle when Azize listed as one of the "secondary theoretical elements" on his list: *"The 'ideal' himself actually exists."* Of course, he exists! First-order beings are immortal within the cosmos. They never go away. They make themselves eternally, graciously available to our beleaguered planet. And that is in fact, in my estimation, precisely the reason this exercise actually works. But let me hold my further comments on this point until somewhat later in this series.

"WHERE PRAYER HAS BEEN PROVEN VALID..."

Remember, however, that you are not trying to directly connect with the ideal himself, but rather to "represent" to yourself the reservoir—foyer—atmosphere of energy generated around the place where that prophet had his chief sphere of operations. While this apparent reluctance to aim higher may or may not finally prove to be a failure of mystical nerve (that's the issue I want to circle back to a bit later), there are nonetheless two excellent practical reasons for placing our attention here. First of all, the experience of a highly-energized atmosphere around a holy place is something that I daresay most of us have actually tasted. Whether it's an ancient church or monastery, the tomb of a saint, the Upper Room in Jerusalem, the sacred river Ganges, or the Kaaba in Mecca where millions of Muslim faithful make hajj—you know that *something* gathers in these places, and this "something" remains available there in an unusually concentrated dose. It hangs in the air as thick as incense in those places "where prayer has been proven valid" (as T. S. Eliot put it), and through it you find your own prayer mysteriously intensified.

So you will probably recognize exactly what Azize is talking about in his first two bullet points on this exercise: "'Higher substances' form certain 'reservoirs' above the earth ... [formed] from emanations and vibrations that arise when people pray to the 'Ideal' who live on the spot of earth immediately below." And at least this gives us a concrete starting point as the other, more "out there" premises on which this exercise is based still go swirling around in our heads.

The other thing that's useful about this focus is that it is so geographically expansive. As you allow right arm–right leg–left arm– left leg to connect with Mecca, India, Jerusalem, and Tibet, you are essentially inviting your body, as it comes into sensation, *to become co-extensive, symbolically with the entire world* ("the four corners of the round earth," in that marvelous image from the poet Christopher Smart). And in our broken and aching world, that is a powerful self-extension, itself a mysterious form of embrace in a world where embracing has suddenly become too scary to even imagine. As you do the familiar body

rotation, but now sensing each of your limbs as somehow connected to a geographical place on the earth and, through the
atmosphere just above it, to its corresponding ideal in worlds
beyond, you may well feel yourself expanded both horizontally
and vertically, becoming momentarily co-extensive not only
with the whole world but with the whole Ray of Creation. Do
not think you have done nothing here. It is a sensation from
which you never emerge unchanged.

3. Representing Mecca

The next important thing to consider as we approach this
exercise is what it means to "*represent something to yourself*," as
you will shortly be asked to do sequentially in this exercise:
for Mecca, India, Jerusalem, and Tibet. What, specifically, does
this entail?

I mentioned in my first pass through this topic (in the
Atmosphere Exercise) that representing something to yourself
is not quite the same as visualizing it. In practical terms, however, it does take a bit of time to get the hang of the difference
between them. *Visualization* is more mental, imagistic, sharp-
edged, and—inasmuch as it remains oriented toward the surface of things—superficial. *Representing* dives below the surface,
is less concerned with the appearance and more with the overall
energetic impression, and is in fact carried more by sensation
than by cognition. A student in the Bennett line of the Work
helpfully clarifies: "The images (Kaaba in Mecca, etc.) are seen
in one's eye at first, but *during contact no mental picture is present.*
We don't contact the mental image—rather, the reservoir of
energy."

You may find it helpful to begin by establishing a strong sensation in the limb itself before introducing any image, or even the place name. As you do introduce your image, do so in the spirit of Thomas Keating's celebrated mantra: "*ever-so-gently, like a feather placed on a ball of cotton.*" Straining or forcing toward a desired effect is not the best way to concentrate. Remember that the real trick is to concentrate your attention not at the objective pole but at the *subjective* one (i.e., at the core of yourself). Then it can flow out effortlessly and brush the object lightly without getting stuck there. (We practiced some of this in the Clear Impressions exercise.)

So instead of frantically trying to conjure up mental images of Mecca or the Taj Mahal—instead, get settled and stable inside yourself, establish sensation in the appointed arm or leg, and when you're ready, gently bring the intended location to mind. Invite it to come "online." You will be surprised how the pieces start to fill in of their own accord. Mecca, Jerusalem, India, Tibet—each come gently to you even if you have never physically been there or studied a tourist brochure, even if you don't know exactly who Lama is or how Muhammed got to Mecca in the first place. Remember, this is an *energy* exchange, not an information exchange. Something deeper than your mind is at work here.

Those of you who have spent time praying with icons may have well some inkling of what this "something deeper" might be—or at least, of the direction in which it lies. The subtle dance that goes on in this practice as you fall into entrainment with an icon is a fairly good analogue to the entrainment that actually undergirds the process of representing. At first, you think you're the one gazing at the icon. But as you allow yourself to be drawn in through its eyes, you begin to get the distinct feeling that the icon is also gazing back at you! Then, as the entrainment grows still deeper, both *you* and *icon* gradually disappear, and you step through the portal it has now become, directly into the cave of your heart.

The key that really unlocked this exercise for me, however, came totally out of left field about twenty years ago, with no direct connection to the exercise at all. It was less than a year after Rafe's death, toward the end of a late fall teaching gig at the Vancouver School of Theology. Still raw in my grief and clinging for dear life to the soul-bond I still sensed between us, I was doing my best to keep his image continually before my mind, fearing that to lose concentration would be to lose the connection. One afternoon as I was walking along the shoreline lost in my usual doleful effort, a sudden catspaw came hurtling across the water, and a voice distinctly Rafe's whispered in my inner ear, "Shhhhhh! You do not have to come all the way to me because I am also coming toward you ..."

Talk about having your head instantly rearranged.

Fundamentally, it's so simple, so very simple. Why, after all, should we imagine that it is only from *our* side that the work is being done, that the water we are endeavoring to draw from those reservoirs is impersonal and mechanical, obedient only to the Newtonian laws that govern the physics of this earth realm? No, we are talking here about a meeting ground, where the highest aspirations of human hearts throughout the ages have met and been graciously received by these higher cosmic servants on the other side *who are also coming toward us* because they love us and are invested in our ultimate flourishing. Mecca does not appear because we conjure it up through our own powers of concentration; it arrives because the Megalocosmos is imbued with intelligence, compassion, and a deep responsivity to our sincere desire for connection. It is the tenderness that evokes it, not the skillfulness.

Even if you don't have a clue how to take this first step into "representing Mecca," take it anyway. Trust. Somehow Mecca will appear.

4. Stepping onto the Bridge

You have now filled your limbs with the energy of those four sacred places: Mecca, India, Jerusalem, Tibet. You should be able at this point to sense your two arms and two legs as fully online, vibrant with sensation. They have become, to use one of Gurdjieff's pet words, "accumulators." And these accumulators are now fully charged and ready to go.

While the term, accumulator, often gets explained as a kind of reservoir, I think the term "battery" actually comes closer to Gurdjieff's intention. Out here on Eagle Island, my two solar panels collect the energy of the sun and store it in four marine batteries, from which it can be drawn (unless there's a prolonged rainy spell) to light my house, run my computer, and send you this post. Exactly the same type of collection and redistribution of energy will be at work as we move into the second part of this exercise.

Remember that the goal here is not to fade out sensation in one limb as you shift your attention to another, but to quietly expand attention so that you can feel the cumulative resonance of all four limbs: your whole body as a single vibratory field. As noted in the Clear Impressions Exercise, "As always, the sensation of the body is cumulative, so that I finally finish up with a total sensation" (#6, Azize, 266).

Now, lean deeply into this total sensation. As I mentioned in my earlier commentary, your body has now become symbolically coextensive with "the four corners of the round earth," and each of your limbs pulses with the subtly different energies of the four great sacred traditions: Islamic, Judeo-Christian, Indian, and Tibetan. If your sensing has become very keen, you may actually be able to pick up these subtly different flavors, but don't push it with your head; it's enough simply to know that these great rivers of human longing are like colors of the rainbow, each one of them bearing a unique vibratory expression of the invisible white light of God.

Savor this moment deeply. Then, when you're ready, step out onto the bridge. Now follows the second part of this exercise. Breathe in air consciously while drawing into yourself the substances accumulated in the limbs so that it can flow to meet the air you are breathing in. It mixes with the air by itself at the level of the breast. Then pour it into the sex organs.

In this relatively brief transition into the second part of the exercise you will be asked to perform three critical operations:

1. to *inhale*, consciously drawing in the substances accumulated in the limbs;
2. during the inhale, *to allow these substances to mix* on their own with the finer substances in the air;
3. to *pour* this mixed substance into your genitals.

We have already practiced all three of these operations separately. Drawing (or "sucking") a substance from the periphery of ourselves into the center was a skill we practiced in the Atmosphere Exercise. Consciously inhaling the finer substances available to us in the air and retaining them for our own inner development is at the heart of the Make Strong Exercise. And the genital placement of your attention has already been introduced in the Clear Impressions Exercise, though in a somewhat more diffuse form ("the area of the sex organs and spine").

How long does this bridge last? The answer, basically, is that "it lasts as long as it lasts." Gurdjieff's intention, clearly, is that this is fundamentally *a single unified gesture*: a drawing in and a pouring out. Symbolically, it is a single breath of timeless time, and the emphasis is so much on the unity of the action that Gurdjieff does not even explicitly state that the "pouring out" occurs on the exhale. This is not an action pasted onto a breathing rhythm; it is a breathing rhythm profoundly in service to an action, an action itself mysteriously suffused with the resonance of a sacred consecration.

Practically speaking, however, you can't afford to float through this moment on autopilot. You need to be *consciously present* to the sensation in your body (particularly to the sensation in your chest, where the mixing of substances is occurring)—which means it may take a few breaths to get your sensation actually up and running in this region of your body. Joseph Azize reports to me that in George Adie's teaching, five breaths was the general rule of thumb in lieu of more specific instructions, but he emphasized that *this is not about counting breaths*, but simply a general indication of the average duration required to bring yourself fully present. Adie also frequently commented that as proficiency in sensing increases, duration tends to decrease.

So, if you wind up crossing this bridge over the course of several breaths, *do you deposit a bit of the substance in your sex organs on each outbreath, or do you make a single final deposit?* This exercise in particular allows for a certain amount of personal experimentation, and I would encourage you to explore a few different combinations and see what inner feedback you get. My own experience is that it wants to remain a single donation: a single moment in which you consciously choose to complete this action and do so. Till then, let your attention remain nested in the sensation of your inbreath as you draw in these extraordinary substances and ready yourself to become even more consciously a crucible of cosmic transformation.

In my next post I will have more to say about the genital placement of this exercise.

5. The Cosmic Mixer

As the second part of this exercise officially gets underway, you are instructed to take the cumulative vibration of those substances now concentrated in your limbs, draw it deeply into your inner core through one or more conscious breaths, then "pour it into the sex organs."

The genital placement of this highly charged subtle energy is admittedly a strong, perhaps even dicey, move. Operationally, it may present some initial discomfort. In the Bennett version of the exercise, the outpouring is in fact directed to the breast rather than to the genitals. This is certainly a more familiar and no doubt more comfortable placement (the Sufis and Hesychasts among you will recognize it well), although it winds up imparting a distinctly different flavor to the final result. Azize argues persuasively that the genital placement is in fact correct, building his case not only on fidelity to the Gurdjieffian original, but on his own detailed research into Gurdjieff's Food Diagram (see: Ouspensky, *In Search of the Miraculous*, Chapter 9) from which he can stipulate clearly what alchemical contribution to the transformation of higher substances is specifically played by these organs. The subject is highly technical and neither necessary nor appropriate to our immediate concern here. But if you are a Gurdjieff "chemical factory" adept and want to see the general direction in which Azize is headed, I would point you toward his note 11 on pages 163–64 of his book.

Meanwhile, your mind is no doubt already picking up the symbolic resonances: "creativity," "fertility," "primordial sexuality." Yes, but try to hold a lid on all this symbolic chatter. It keeps the mind overinvolved and overstimulated, which will get in the way of your work. Instead, stay quietly gathered in sensation and allow yourself to be gently led into this mysterious new terrain. You will be touching on secrets that monastic anchorites and sannyasi have come to know throughout the ages.

Having deposited this energy in your genitals, the next step is to move it to seven specific regions of your own body, working from bottom to top using the familiar I AM pattern. On the *I*—always on the inhale—you connect with your genital accumulator. On the *AM*—the exhale—you distribute this energy sequentially to right leg, left leg, lower abdomen, entire abdomen, torso, both arms and shoulders, and head.

The means by which this connection and distribution occurs, is of course, through your capacity *to move sensation by means of your attention*. It is the fundamental skill underlying all these Gurdjieff exercises, which we have been practicing from the very start.

ENCORE, I AM

It may be helpful to review some of the earlier comments I have made about the *I AM* in the Lord Have Mercy and Make Strong exercises. There is an instruction commonly given in Gurdjieffian practice to "*feel* the I and *sense* the AM"—or in other words, to approach the *I* through the feeling (or emotional) center and the *AM* through sensation. This placement flows seamlessly into feeling the *I* as your most primordial sense of your own finite particularity and the *AM* as the undifferentiated simple, infinite *Presence*. And *voilà,* there we are back again on the cusp of "the innermost mystery of the ontopoietic (self-manifesting) process," to return again to Olga Louchakova's extraordinary insight. (See: my commentary on the Lord Have Mercy Exercise, section 3). Or as Thomas Keating put it more simply at the very end of his life:

> When there is no more "me, myself, or mine."
> Only "I AM" remains
> Then the "I" may fall away,
> Leaving just the "AM" (Keating, *The Secret Embrace*, vol. 1, poem VI, "Out of Nothing").

It is that rhythmic intercirculation—that "secret embrace" between the finite and infinite—which ultimately comprises "The Mercy of God" and links the two expressions, "Lord have mercy" and "I AM" inextricably together. In this exercise you have leaned deeply into that mystery and breathed in some of its boundless fecundity.

SHAKE IT UP, SHARE IT AROUND

Notice how this exercise is a total energetic mix-up! In at least three ways you have ingested and recombined separate elements:

1. You have taken four separate sacred traditions (Islamic, Judeo-Christian, Hindu-Buddhist, and Tibetan Buddhist) and allowed their energies to flow together in your own being.
2. You have further mixed these energies (technically, these subtle "substances") with the air itself at the level of the breast, mindful that this air itself contains fine substances coming from other planetary realms along the Ray of Creation.

3. You have drawn this recombined mix into your genitals, then redistributed it through the various regions of your own body. Limbs that formerly served as accumulators for specific sacred traditions are now flooded with the combined and fortified vibrancy of the whole.

4. And you have used this to strengthen and accelerate your own transformation, in order to better equip you to offer yourself back into that whole in order to "lighten the sorrow of our Common Father."

If you feel like you've just become a conscious fractal of that great "*Trogoautoegocrat*" —that intercosmic dance of reciprocal feeding that maintains the entire Ray of Creation in its dynamic equilibrium—guess what? *You have!* No wonder your whole being is reverberating.

A final operational note. Gurdjieff emphasizes that when you have completed the exercise, "rest ten or fifteen minutes in a collected state, not [allowing] thought or feeling or organic instinct to pass outside the limits of the atmosphere of the body." In such a way, what you have so preciously collected here will not be simply dissipated but can be offered back through that web of atmospheres, directly back to the planet, and in fact to the entire Ray of Creation.

6. Stealing?

Gurdjieff did in fact sometimes refer to the Four Ideals Exercise as "the Stealing Exercise." I wish I could say he was just being playful, but I don't think he was. The conviction that "the Ideal himself is too far [beyond] for an unprepared man to be able to enter into contact with him" remains an obdurate and troubling aspect of Gurdjieff's teaching (Azize, 231.) To his way of picturing the situation, it would seem that the best we mere mortals can do is to offer up our prayers and devotion. But even these are able to rise only so far toward their intended recipient and remain trapped within the planetary atmosphere, where they form concentrated pockets above the immediate geographical regions from which they originate. These constitute the foyers, or reservoirs, we have been working with in this exercise—Mecca, Jerusalem, India, Tibet—to which we are invited to put out an imaginal umbilical cord and siphon off some the spiritual energy concentrated here for our own personal development.

Not only is this questionable theology from a Christian standpoint, but I believe it also betrays Gurdjieff's own highest understanding, implicit in his majestic and heart-expanding vision of the Great Trogoautoegocrat, the intricate web of reciprocal nurturance that holds the entire Ray of Creation in dynamic equilibrium.

I do not need to climb onto my Christian soapbox and start citing reconciliation theology ("In Christ heaven and earth have been brought together, God and man have been reconciled, all things hold together.") in order to state the obvious. It is known universally, in every religion, that these great cosmic servants do not simply vanish into the stratosphere but are distinguishable by *their intimate proximity*—their willingness, even their seeming delight, to move toward us and meet us where we are. The testimony by countless numbers of Christians of personal encounters with Jesus is matched by the experience of devout Sufis and Hindus at the tombs of their respective saints. I have visited some of these Sufi tombs and can attest that these saints do indeed show up, each bearing his or her own distinctive fragrance. And in fact, in the Indian tradition the name for the tomb of a Hindu saint—*samadhi*—is identical to the term used to describe the experience of bliss. All along the Ray of Creation *we are met*, and the sense of intimacy and interaccessibility suffuses the entire cosmos. There is nothing that cannot be penetrated by love—no realm too high, no heart too darkened. And love moves in all directions along the Ray—not simply rung-by-rung on an interrealmic monkey bar but leapfrogging across worlds to wherever it is beckoned. Gurdjieff's insistence that the direct vibrational presence of the Holy Sun Absolute grows increasingly attenuated as we move down the Ray of Creation (becoming, by the time it reaches our own realm essentially imperceptible) seems to me a curiously Newtonian holdover from classic "Great Chain of Being" redshift metaphysics. The Einstein in him, I am convinced, knew better.

So these four holy places we have been working with in this exercise cannot be construed simply as glorified cosmic locker rooms where the faithful breathe in the sweat of their own spiritual exertions. They are in fact *imaginal transfer stations* where exchange between the realms is going on at an extremely high order of intensity and potency. Something is indeed being bestowed here *from above*: blessing, miracle, samadhi, revelation, fortification for the road ahead. But something is being bestowed here *from below* as well. The fruits of our "conscious labor and intentional suffering" are not merely the crystallization within ourselves of those "subtle being bodies" that confer immortality and agency within higher realms. They are also, as Saint Paul precisely realized, "love, joy, peace, forbearance, kindness, faithfulness, gentleness, and self-control." These alchemized fruits of the awakened heart, ground in the crucible of our human marrow and our human longing, are then offered back up into the Ray, where they indeed become "food for the Gods." And for our own starving earth as well.

As William Segal, a first-generation Gurdjieff student, points out in his essay, "The Force of Attention":

> Just as man's structure needs to be vivified by the infusion of finer vibrations, those very same vibrations require the mixing of coarse material for their maintenance. Without the upward transmission of energies through the intermediary of conscious attention, the universe would give in to entropy.

It is a two-way street. There is giving, and there is receiving going on in these imaginal transfer stations. There is *exchange*. The Mercy of God. ...

To my mind, *this* is Gurdjieff's own highest theology, against which the innuendo of "stealing" must finally be laid to rest. One cannot steal what is freely given. One cannot steal what is sacrificially offered, perhaps imperfectly, but with sincerity and mystical courage.

And that, for me, is also the key to unlocking the mysterious power and cosmic tenderness coiled within this Four Ideals Exercise. I will have more to say on it in my final post.

7. The Ocean and the Drop

"Man is a microcosm," the ancient philosophers continually reminded us. In the vernacular of our own times, we would more likely say we are a *fractal* of the whole, a *hologram*. We are a tiny slice—a single pixel of consciousness —that recapitulates in perfect proportion the pattern of the entire whole.

We can beam this holographic capacity in either of two directions. We can zoom our consciousness vastly outwards until we become coextensive with the entire created order. We can experience ourselves as a single drop in a vast ocean of cosmic aliveness. Or we can zoom it daringly inward and experience the whole ocean in the conscious drop that we are.

What I find so exhilarating about the Four Ideals Exercise is that it invites (actually *requires*) us to do both: to become both the drop-in-the-ocean and the-ocean-in-a-drop in a single, flowing motion that is powerful and mysteriously sacramental. We play ourselves like an accordion whose keyboard is the Ray of Creation.

ZOOM OUT

The first part of the exercise catapults you into that vast expansion. As you connect with Mecca, Jerusalem, India, Tibet, you can literally feel your body becoming coextensive with "the four corners of the round earth." And the expansion is not only lateral but vertical as well, as successive realms along the Ray of Creation begin to open up within you. Those four "atmospheres" hovering over their respective holy places are in fact *those places themselves as they are actually embodied in the imaginal realm,* and the work in this first part of the exercise is situated powerfully at the point of exchange between imaginal and earthly reality. That is why it is so important not to simply "push through" the imaginal ranks of the faithful and attempt to connect directly with the Ideal himself. That connection is always there and instantly accessible, but *the real sacramental and collective work in this exercise is in fact powerfully concentrated at that imaginal junction point.* This is the epicenter of what Gurdjieff called "the conscious circle of humanity." It is here that earth-healing is concentrated. Here that the mystical body, "the world soul," is built up. Don't push through this realm too quickly. It is in solidarity with our brothers and sisters throughout the ages that our world will be pulled through its present crisis.

Once you give yourself permission to regard these imaginal foyers not as *checkpoints* but as *meeting points*, you do indeed feel the nurturance flowing to you from realms still more subtle. The "finer elements emanating from the sun" pour into your lungs as you consciously breathe them in. The adamantine presence of the Ideals themselves leans and harkens toward you from realms still higher—till at last you can even pick up the distant reverberations of that primordial "secret embrace" between the Manifest and Unmanifest from which the entire created order emerges. If you are quiet enough and steady enough, you can become coextensive with the entire Ray of Creation. Like a vast concert organ, octaves upon octaves of celestial harmony pulsate through your being as you do indeed come to grasp "how wide and long and high and deep" is this ocean of Mercy, and—as Saint Paul so boldly promises in his celebrated teaching in Ephesians 3:19—"to be filled with the very nature of God."

ZOOM IN

Then just as quickly, in the second part of the exercise you rein this vastness in, draw it into your own tiny pixel of being and breathe it into the microcosm of your body for the deep nurturance of your own conscious pixel-hood. The ocean pours into the drop. You are being fed from worlds beyond worlds: angels; archangels; "the communion of saints"; the conscious circle of humanity; the vast stream of living souls past, present and yet to come. And curling beneath your feet, awaiting the time when the life force coiled within you will be returned to them (either by your physical death or your conscious rebirth): earth, plants, the biosphere, the geosphere—the entire great *Megalocosmos*—tumbling and turning in this grand dance of reciprocal feeding.

The "coinherence," British mystic Charles Williams called

it. The profound, mutual indwelling of the entire created order. In the Four Ideals Exercise, you get to taste a fractal of that coinherence. The fractal that you imperishably are.

"AGIOS Ô THEOS"

Touching on elements of both Tonglen and Eucharist, this exercise is implicitly sacramental in resonance. In the Tibetan practices of Tonglen, conscious breathing is combined with substituted love as you intentionally breathe in the pain or suffering of another and offer your own body as a place of cleansing. In Eucharist, this same substituted love (a.k.a. *exchange!*) continues to glow brightly, and you experience the same accordion-like dance between the micro and the macro as you take Christ's body into our own, only to find yourself simultaneously ingested into his own mystical body. The resonances are strong enough to alert us that we are on holy ground here. In its own way, the Four Ideals Exercise is equally a "Mass on the World," even out-Teilharding Teilhard in its grandeur and scale. Our own finite pixel becomes the "body and blood" consciously offered up on the altar of the Great Trogoautoegocrat, then returned to us sanctified, overflowing with a strength and tenderness not our own, but ours to offer back, "for the life of the world."

The ocean of Mercy flowing into the drop.

The drop flowing into the ocean of Mercy.

The Great Trogoautoegocrat.

The Four Ideals.

"Lord, have mercy …"

8. Vertical Exchange

One final point to keep in mind as we tackle the Four Ideals Exercise. The web extends not merely horizontally, but *vertically* as well. It also serves as a conduit for *exchange between the realms*.

The world's sacred traditions unanimously teach that there are other realms beyond our own—several higher, a few lower—each one furnishing a different set of conditions for the manifestation of divine creativity. Our own Christian notion of heaven and hell is an attenuated version of what has more broadly unfolded on the great cosmological roadmaps as the Great Chain of Being. These maps depict an elaborate procession of worlds within worlds, stretching from the unfathomable abyss of the Divine Unmanifest through progressively more variegated densities—angelic, causal, imaginal, material—until it finally meets its endpoint in total density in what ancient cosmologists called "outer darkness" and contemporary cosmologists call a "black hole."

To this elaborate roadmap Gurdjieff adds an all-important new twist. In his Ray of Creation (his equivalent for the Great Chain of Being), the energy does not simply stream out from the divine center in a continuous cosmic redshift. Something is returned as well. Each realm has a contribution to make to the well-being of its neighbors, so that along the entire Ray, energy is not only lost but also gained. Entropy does not have the final word. Instead, the whole manifest universe becomes a single, gigantic *self-specifying system*, maintaining its dynamic equilibrium through the continuous exchange among its parts. Gurdjieff gives this process the jaw-busting name Trogoautoegocrat ("I keep myself alive by eating"), but you can also just call it *reciprocal feeding*.

This is of course the crucial piece of information that

dropped off our post-Enlightenment roadmaps, both sacred and secular. Its disappearance largely accounts for the blind arrogance that led the human species into ecological catastrophe but leaves us still able to pull ourselves out. We're working with a map that's far too small, that leaves us still unable to fathom our solemn accountability within the vast scheme of things. As Gurdjieff forcefully reiterates, it is only within the full breadth of this great cosmological exchange that human beings can ever come to discover their true purpose and dignity.

HELP FROM ABOVE

The bottom line here is that we do indeed receive help "from above," and we are expected to *give* help as well, not only to our own realm but to higher realms as well. The miracle is that we can actually do this.

The realm just above ours, widely known as the "imaginal" has long been seen as the nexus for this exchange between the realms. It has traditionally been understood as the realm of prophecy, dreams, visions, and subtle inner guidance. The closest Christian rendition of this idea lies in the Communion of Saints, with its underlying conviction that these attained beings are somehow still out there and willing to give help. This is no magical illusion. It is a vestigial remembrance of the true state of things, a remembrance which thankfully refuses to die in the human heart.

Gurdjieff's own version of this teaching is found in his notion of a "conscious circle of humanity." Bridging the so-called "abyss" of death, there extends a chain of conscious human beings—some still in bodily form, some on the other side—united by the common denominator of their conscious work. They are the imaginal continuation of the human web, and their chain extends all the way across the imaginal realm to the threshold of realms still higher, from which the greatest of the cosmic servants descend. Along this entire chain of hearts (truly, organically, a great chain of *beings*), the uploading and downloading goes on intensely. Here on the human side we indeed receive wisdom, help, guidance, as well as sudden surprising infusions of clarity and force. And we offer back the fruits of our conscious work in the form of forbearance, gentleness, joy, peace, generosity, compassion—those perennial "fruits of the spirit" through which not only our own planetary atmosphere but the entire Ray of Creation is warmed. It is our consummate human alchemy.

My own teacher, Rafe, was mesmerized by this vision of a conscious circle of humanity. He yearned more than anything to be a part of it, and he saw his own final life task as preparing me to take my place in that chain as well and hold up my end on this side once he had physically left the planet. I am quite certain he made it across and that his conscious service goes on in higher realms. As for myself, I have often felt in these twenty-five years since his death like the cabin boy left to steer the schooner, but I have done the best I could to stay the course and to stay true to what he taught me.

I do know the vital importance of keeping this line of inter-realmic exchange open, particularly at this crucial juncture in our planetary history. There is simply not enough spaciousness, breadth, hope, love, empowerment, or real juice left in the visions of either our secular or traditionally religious roadmaps. We cannot *think* our way out of this mess, and we can no longer even *imagine* our way out since establishment religion has long ago sold its mystical birthright for a mess of pseudo-psychological pottage. Only in that deeper listening will the way be found again.

Passion and compassion are still there to rekindle us.

Our planet is infinitely precious and lovingly tended by those "higher being bodies" in worlds above. We humans are a crucial link in the great Trogoautoegocrat, and we will find our footing once again. But this will come to pass as there are those who have learned to listen deeply into that great cosmic web and are able both to receive and offer back the food that comes to us from above.

Acknowledgments

A sincere thank you to all my Wisdom students worldwide who took on these exercises, worked with them with brilliance and integrity, and "warmed the atmosphere" of our frightened and broken planet.

A special thanks to Joseph Azize for graciously allowing these six exercises to be shared within the confines of our Wisdom Community Facebook page, and for his support and judicious guidance.

To the ever-intrepid Paul Cohen for his willingness to publish these commentaries and expedite the timeline so that the material remained timely; and to Dory Mayo for her careful and clear editorial oversight.

About the Author

Cynthia Bourgeault is a modern-day mystic, Episcopal priest, and theologian. She is a core faculty member at the Center for Action and Contemplation and founding director of an international network of Wisdom Schools. She is the author of numerous books, including *The Wisdom Jesus*, *The Holy Trinity and the Law of Three*, and *Eye of the Heart: A Spiritual Journey into the Imaginal Realm*.

Printed in the USA
CPSIA information can be obtained
at www.ICGtesting.com
LVHW051832071123
763187LV00007B/1068